Curriculum Studies
in the Lifelong Learning Sector

Curriculum Studies
in the Lifelong Learning Sector

Jonathan Tummons

LearningMatters

First published in 2009 by Learning Matters Ltd
Reprinted in 2010

British Library Cataloguing in Publication Data
A CIP record for this book is available from the British Library.

ISBN: 978 1 84445 193 7

Cover design by Topics – The Creative Partnership
Project management by Deer Park Productions, Tavistock, Devon
Typeset by PDQ Typesetting Ltd, Newcastle under Lyme
Printed and bound in Great Britain by Bell & Bain Ltd, Glasgow

Learning Matters
33 Southernhay East
Exeter EX1 1NX
Tel: 01392 215560
info@learningmatters.co.uk
www.learningmatters.co.uk

Contents

The author

Jonathan Tummons has worked in higher education since 1995, when he first began teaching at the University of Leeds. He took up a post as senior lecturer in education at the University of Teesside after six years as a lecturer in teacher education in the FE sector. As a consultant, he has contributed to programmes for schools broadcast by Channel 4. Jonathan is currently completing an ESRC-funded PhD at the University of Lancaster, researching the assessment of trainee teachers in the learning and skills sector. As well as publishing articles in various journals and edited collections, he is the author of *Assessing Learning in the Lifelong Learning Sector* and *Becoming a Professional Tutor in the Lifelong Learning Sector*, both published by Learning Matters.

Acknowledgements

I should like to thank a small number of people who have helped me think and talk about things at different times: Paul Ashwin, John Aston, Liz Atkins, Suzanne Blake, Jane Brooke, Judy Hallam, Mary Hamilton, Gaynor Mount, Kevin Orr, Nena Skrbic, Sue Wallace. I'd also like to say thanks to my BA Education and Training students, who have made Tuesday nights at Leeds Thomas Danby a particular pleasure for me this academic year. Thanks are also due to Julia Morris. And especially Jo, Alex and Eleanor.

I should also like to thank the following for permission given to reproduce material in this book: Professor Stephen Ball; Sage Publications Ltd; Taylor and Francis Books Ltd.

Every effort has been made to trace the copyright holders and to obtain their permission for the use of copyright material. The publisher and author will gladly receive information enabling them to rectify any error or omission in subsequent editions.

Introduction

This book is intended to help all those who are currently working towards a teaching qualification that is accredited by Lifelong Learning UK (LLUK). You may already be working as a teacher or trainer in a further education college, and studying for your professional qualifications on a part-time, in-service basis. Alternatively, you may be studying for your qualification on a full-time basis, and may be about to embark on, or already engaged on, a teaching placement. You may be employed, or seeking employment, as a tutor in adult or community education, provided by a local education authority or by organisations such as the Workers' Educational Association (WEA). You may be working as a trainer or instructor in the health sector, or in the police or fire services. These varied contexts are all covered by the LLUK standards, and practitioners in these areas are all eligible for LLUK accreditation.

This is not primarily a theoretical work. Curriculum studies is an area of significant theoretical and philosophical study: this book is not intended to be part of that particular body of literature. However, there are a few occasions when a focus on current research is desirable, and the references provided will allow those with a taste for theory to explore further. Essentially, this book is intended to provoke action as well as thought: the activities within this book, often underpinned by case studies that are composite forms of real-life experiences that I have encountered in adult education centres, further education colleges and in community-based education and training settings, are designed to facilitate the application of the ideas and issues discussed in the real world of the teacher or trainer.

Meeting National Standards

From 1 January 2005 a new organisation, Lifelong Learning UK (LLUK), began operating as the body responsible for – amongst other things – the professional development of all employees in the field of lifelong learning. It is LLUK that is responsible for the new occupational standards that appear in this book.

How to use this book

This book may be read from cover to cover, in one sitting, or it may be read on a chapter-by-chapter basis over a longer period of time. Each chapter is designed so that it can be read in isolation, as and when needed, although references to topics covered in other chapters will be found from time to time.

Within each chapter, the reader will find a number of features that are designed to engage the reader, and provoke an active response to the ideas and themes that are covered. Objectives at the start of each chapter set the scene, and then the appropriate LLUK professional standards for that chapter are listed. In some places, an activity will be found. These activities have been specially designed to facilitate the practical application of some of the issues covered. The case studies and real-life examples that are to be found in this book are drawn from a variety of different teaching and training contexts, as a reflection of the diversity of the learning and skills sector as a whole. Finally, each chapter finishes with suggestions for what to do next. A small number of sources, books, journal articles and websites are recommended at the end of each chapter. These lists are by no means exhaustive. Featured items have been chosen because of their suitability and value for use and study by trainee teachers in the learning and skills sector.

Learning, and reading this book

My own research is focused on how trainee teachers in the learning and skills sector make sense of the assessment requirements that they have to meet while studying for their teacher training qualifications. From this perspective, as well as from my perspective as a teacher educator, I have radically changed my own ideas about what I think learning is, and how it can be made to happen. This book is not an appropriate venue for me to set forth my own views, but one or two comments are, I feel, necessary. Firstly, a general point: I think that learning can happen in all kinds of places and at all kinds of times, and it never really stops. Learning happens as a consequence of our social actions: talking to colleagues or friends; going to work; finding ways to deal with dilemmas that we have not encountered before. In this book, I have tried to set out some themes and ideas that can seem to be quite remote and theoretical, and to situate them firmly within the working lives of tutors.

Secondly, a more specific point: I think that language needs to be used carefully. There is a lot of jargon in teacher education and despite my efforts and assurances, many of the trainees with whom I have worked still resist it. In this book, I have tried to cut the use of jargon to a minimum. There is a place for it: the right words can say in a small amount of space what might otherwise take a long time. There are also, in teacher education, a number of books and articles that are sometimes a little forbidding to the reader, especially to those for whom teacher training is a first experience of higher education. I have tried to keep this reader in mind, while at the same time providing sufficient depth for the more academically experienced reader.

I am always happy to hear from trainee teachers about my writing or my research and to receive offers from trainees who would be willing to help.

1
Defining curriculum

By the end of this chapter you should:

- be able to evaluate definitions of curriculum, according to context;
- know and be able to apply relevant definitions of curriculum, as appropriate to your own professional practice;
- be able to begin a critical evaluation of your own curriculum, in terms of how it is delivered in the classroom and how it is experienced by the students with whom you work.

Professional Standards

This chapter relates to the following Professional Standards:

Professional Values:

DS 1 Planning to promote equality, support diversity and to meet the aims and learning needs of learners.

DS 2 Learner participation in the planning of learning.

Professional Knowledge and Understanding:

DK 2.1 The importance of including learners in the planning process.

Professional Practice:

DP 1.1 Plan coherent and inclusive learning programmes that meet learners' needs and curriculum requirements, promote equality and engage with diversity effectively.

This chapter will allow you to work towards the following elements of the *LLUK Minimum Core*:
Language and Literacy – Personal Language Skills
Reading:

- **Find, and select from, a range of reference material and sources of information, including the internet.**
- **Use and reflect on a range of reading strategies to interpret texts and to locate information or meaning.**
- **Identify and record the key information or messages contained within reading material using note-taking techniques.**

Introduction

A book called 'Curriculum Studies in the Lifelong Learning Sector' would, you might think, be able to provide a straightforward definition of 'curriculum' for the reader at, or near, the very start. I have lost count of the number of times when I have told my teacher-training students, while they are completing assignments, to provide proper definitions, accompanied by an appropriate reference and perhaps a quotation, for terms such as 'socially situated learning' or 'behaviourism'. While I always encourage my students to work from a variety of text-books, rather than just one, these definitions tend to be pretty uniform. By this I mean that with occasional minor variations, different authors tend to use the terms 'socially situated learning' or 'behaviourism' in similar ways, reflecting the fact that the meanings attached to these terms are pretty much consensual. (Just to be sure, and for the benefit of the curious, I have included definitions of these two terms at the end of this chapter.)

When my students have to work on their curriculum module assignments, however, this simple act of defining terms becomes somewhat complicated. The variations in the definitions that they read seem to be significantly greater, and therefore less straightforward, than they are used to. Moreover, the word 'curriculum' is invariably prefixed by an additional word – 'vocational', 'total', 'hidden' – that raises further questions. Sometimes, the word 'curriculum', on its own, seems too broad, vague or far-reaching to be useful, while combinations like 'enacted curriculum' and 'teaching curriculum' only apply in quite specific contexts. If researchers and writers cannot always agree on what 'curriculum' actually means, then how can we have 'curriculum studies'?

There are several ways to think about this. The simplest response is to begin by looking in a dictionary and then comparing this definition with the working definitions of 'curriculum' that we, as teachers and trainers, carry around in our heads and use when we talk to our colleagues and our students. Then we can start to look at how the word 'curriculum' has been defined and explored over time by different education theorists and researchers, before going on to think about the extent to which these more academic definitions impact on our everyday understanding. And finally we can accept the fact that it is a slippery word, and that the reason why we have 'studies' about it is because there are lots of ways of thinking about it.

PRACTICAL TASK PRACTICAL TASK PRACTICAL TASK PRACTICAL TASK PRACTICAL TASK

Before reading on, write down your own working definition of 'curriculum'. You may wish to discuss this with fellow teacher-training students, or with your mentor or line manager. In addition, spend some time thinking about the different places, or contexts, that you have seen the word used. This might be in a college or adult education centre prospectus, a newsletter from an exam board or an awarding body, a government publication or a funding body report. If you have ready access to materials such as these, make notes of how these different publications use the term, and what the term implies.

Think about where your definition of curriculum comes from. We are not born with definitions of curriculum already present in our heads. Rather, we form our own understanding of the word as a consequence of taking part in conversations, reading how the word has been used, or listening to something on television or radio. To what extent has your working definition been shaped by day-to-day life, as distinct from what might be termed your professional or academic experience?

Defining 'curriculum'

The *Oxford English Dictionary* (*OED*) defines curriculum as:
> *a course; specifically, a regular course of study or training, as at a school or university.*

And for the purposes of this book, we might add the words 'or college' to the end of the above sentence.

The *OED* goes on to give examples of the use of the word, in an educational context, that date back to the seventeenth century. And this is, broadly speaking, the definition that my teacher-training students tend to give when asked to do so. There are a small number of other terms that have been, and continue to be, used synonymously with curriculum: 'programme', 'provision' and 'syllabus', for example. The dictionary definition implies that the curriculum is public (that is to say, it is easily accessible and out in the open, and not concealed in any way), easily identifiable and probably written down somewhere (usually in the handbooks and documents that are supplied by awarding bodies). It appears to be unproblematic and readily accepted throughout different educational sectors. The *OED* definition can, in summary, be said to be straightforward, easily recognisable, and longstanding. So why have so many researchers and writers spent so much time redefining the word?

Refining and redefining 'curriculum'

The problem with 'curriculum', and by extension the main shortcoming of the *OED* definition, is that it leaves lots of unanswered questions behind. Partly this is due to the simple fact that a dictionary definition of just a sentence or two is almost bound to be restricted or limited: there is simply not enough room to debate the ambiguities or nuances that the word generates. To be fair, this is not the responsibility of the dictionary's compilers. And partly this is due to the fact that the dictionary definition in turn rests on some important ideas, while missing out others altogether.

For example, consider the implications of a simple term: 'a course'. In an educational setting, we talk about courses all of the time, but they are hardly uniform in terms of purpose or shape or content. By this I mean that when as teachers and trainers we talk about 'a course', we could be referring to more than one thing. Does the course in question last for ten weeks, six months or two years? Does the student or apprentice attend college once a week, or on a daily basis? Does the student physically attend the course at all, or does he or she participate on a virtual basis, via an e-learning platform? Does the course consist of just one subject or area of interest or specialism, or are several different topics or competencies covered? How are these different topics related to each other, if at all?

A brief survey of the ways in which the word 'curriculum' is used serves to highlight this concern relating to definitions. From looking through a few books, prospectuses and policy documents, a number of different uses of the word quickly emerge. Some are easily recognisable, if not directly relevant to the learning and skills sector: the 'National Curriculum', for example. Others are more pertinent to a QTLS award and therefore deserve further investigation. Partly this is due to the fact that they will help us explore the term 'curriculum'; and partly this is due to the fact that this exploration will allow us to introduce some of the themes of enquiry that will be returned to in more depth in the later chapters of this book. The three examples that we shall begin with are:

1. the Adult Literacy and Numeracy Core Curriculum;
2. the vocational curriculum;
3. the motor vehicle curriculum.

1. The Adult Literacy and Numeracy Core Curriculum

The Adult Literacy and Numeracy Core Curriculum is the end result of a process that can be traced back to the publication of *A Fresh Start*: *Improving Literacy and Numeracy*. This report is also often referred to as the *Moser Report,* after Sir Claus Moser, chair of the Basic Skills Agency, who was appointed chair of a working group investigating post-school basic skills in 1998 by the then Secretary of State for Education, David Blunkett. *A Fresh Start,* published a year later, gave a bleak assessment of literacy and numeracy skills among adults:

> Something like one adult in five in this country is not functionally literate and far more people have problems with numeracy. This is a shocking situation and a sad reflection on past decades of schooling. It is one of the reasons for relatively low productivity in our economy, and it cramps the lives of millions of people. We owe it to them to remedy at public expense the shortcomings of the past. To do so should be a priority for Government, and for all those, in the business world or elsewhere, who can help.
>
> (www.lifelonglearning.co.uk/mosergroup/)

In 2000, the Qualifications and Curriculum Authority (QCA) published national standards for adult literacy and numeracy. These national standards, together with the QCA specifications for key skills units in communications and application of number, all contributed to the creation of the core curriculum, which consists of a number of elements.

> It sets out the entitlement to learning for all adults who have difficulties with literacy and numeracy. It describes the content of what should be taught in literacy and numeracy programmes in: further and adult education; the workplace and programmes for the unemployed; prisons; community-based and family literacy and numeracy programmes. It assists teachers to meet the individual needs of adults through the selection and teaching of skills appropriate to those adults' needs.
>
> (www.dcsf.gov.uk/curriculum_literacy/intro/core/)

The Adult Literacy and Numeracy Core Curriculum can, therefore, be seen as a centrally controlled curriculum, driven in part by government legislation. Actual courses vary in terms of delivery pattern and intensity: a brief look through any local adult education prospectus will quickly highlight any number of different literacy and numeracy courses for adults which may be delivered at a large FE college, an adult education centre or in the workplace. In this example the term 'curriculum' refers to the overall provision of education in literacy and numeracy for a specified student group, delivered in a variety of modes and across a variety of institutional sites, but all nonetheless following a strong central lead.

2. The vocational curriculum

The vocational curriculum is a broad term that is in some ways best approached from the point of view of what it is not. It is invariably found coupled with, or perhaps opposed to, the term 'academic curriculum'. That is to say, it refers in the very broadest terms to education and training provision that pertains to vocational occupations, as delivered in FE colleges and increasingly (through initiatives such as the Increased Flexibility Programme) in schools as well. Courses in areas such as hairdressing, beauty therapy, catering, construction and engineering are typical of the vocational curriculum. By contrast, the academic curriculum tends to be defined in terms of courses in subjects such as mathematics, history, modern languages, sociology and chemistry. As an educational construct, the vocational curriculum can be seen at work in both colleges and the workplace. That is to say, the vocational curriculum is in some sense delivered or assessed in both formal educational settings such as FE colleges or private training centres, and less formal educational settings such as factory floors or workshops. In both settings, however, there is an assumption that formal education or training processes are taking place. The ways in which people learn through informal processes in workplaces tend to be theorised quite differently in terms of both how learning happens and what, and where, the curriculum is.

Rather like the Adult Literacy and Numeracy Core Curriculum, the vocational curriculum has been subject to considerable reorganisation and revision over recent years. Some brief examples will suffice to show these processes at work. National Vocational Qualifications (NVQs), as originally introduced by the National Council for Vocational Qualifications (NCVQ, formed in 1986), were originally intended to be delivered in the workplace, not in educational establishments. Six years later, in 1992, General National Vocational Qualifications (GNVQs) were introduced within colleges. At the time of writing this book, GNVQs have now been phased out completely, after a three-year process, to be replaced by other vocational qualifications such as BTEC Certificates and Diplomas. And some NVQ qualifications are now delivered in colleges, using simulations to replicate working practices where appropriate. At the time of writing this book, the first of the new 14–19 Diplomas are due to be rolled out in the next academic year, representing the latest significant change in the way that the vocational curriculum is delivered and assessed. Nor are these the only such examples of wholesale change to the structure of the vocational curriculum and to vocational qualifications in recent times: we shall return to this theme in Chapter 3.

The vocational curriculum can, therefore, be seen as a complex and fluid entity, catering for the training and education needs of a highly diverse body of students who work within a variety of qualification schemes in a variety of institutional contexts. In this example, the term 'curriculum' refers to all of those courses, programmes, subjects or topics that make up the overall provision of vocational education and training, as distinct from academic or professional courses or programmes of study.

3. The motor vehicle curriculum

The term 'motor vehicle curriculum' relates quite specifically to that area of training provision that pertains to the motor vehicle industry. That is to say, courses and qualifications based on the relevant national occupational standards that have been drawn up by the Institute of the Motor Industry (IMI), the Sector Skills Council for the motor industry, make up the motor vehicle curriculum. In total, there are 25 Sector Skills Councils (SSCs), each representing a different area of industry or business. They have quite a broad remit that includes addressing the skills gaps that are found in some areas of the economy, and working with other stakeholders to improve learning. SSCs play an important role in the current 14–19 curriculum reform agenda, including the creation of the new 14–19 Diplomas, and drawing up national occupational standards, which the new qualifications will need to meet. As such, all SSCs, including the IMI, can be seen as key stakeholders in the curriculum. We shall return to the role of SSCs in the curriculum, and of industry more generally, in Chapter 3.

Within the motor vehicle curriculum there are a range of different courses and qualifications that can be taken: NVQs at different levels, Apprenticeships and Advanced Apprenticeships are all available. Subject areas include vehicle fitting, vehicle maintenance and repair, vehicle body and paint operations and roadside assistance and recovery. The content and assessment strategy of the qualifications are mapped onto the national occupational standards, which ensures that the qualifications are up to date and relevant for the needs of the industry, represented in this process by the IMI.

The motor vehicle curriculum can, therefore, be seen as being quite clearly demarcated within the vocational curriculum as a whole. The motor vehicle curriculum is a specific area of training and assessing activity, with clearly defined outcomes, standards and required areas of competence and expertise. In this example, the term 'curriculum' refers quite narrowly to one area of industrial or technical training: that area of training that is required for a career within the motor vehicle industry, and which representatives of that industry help to design and maintain.

Conclusions

So how can we make sense of these three examples, and the ways in which the term 'curriculum' is used? In only the third example, the motor vehicle curriculum, does the *OED* definition that we started with seem to work without too much difficulty, whereas the Adult Literacy and Numeracy Curriculum seems to be too broad in scope to be described as 'a course'. And the vocational curriculum is broader still. They all refer to particular areas of knowledge, competence or expertise, but in very different ways. So it would seem to be the case that the meaning of the term relies heavily on the context within which it is used. Nor is it too difficult to ascertain the exact meaning of the word from a context within which we might find it. In addition to the three examples already given, we might also include:

- the National Curriculum;
- the Adult ESOL Core Curriculum;
- the History Curriculum;
- the Electrical Installation Curriculum;
- the Early Years Curriculum;
- Curriculum 2000;
- the 14–19 Curriculum.

These examples show, in a similar manner to our three in-depth case studies, how 'curriculum' can refer to both single subject areas, broader areas of provision, and even policy initiatives. They are all very different from each other: some are vocational, others are academic; some refer to single subjects; others refer to whole groups of subjects; some imply particular age ranges, backgrounds or profiles of the intended participants, others do not. Some rest on broader policy changes, and others are very much shaped by industrial requirements. But each one is a kind of curriculum.

REFLECTIVE TASK

Defining curriculum

Refer back to your earlier working definition of curriculum. Does it accommodate the different uses of the term that have been explored above? Reflect on how the use of the word varies. What is implied by the word 'curriculum' in terms of subject matters, intended participants and other stakeholders, in the examples that are given above? Think about how 'curriculum' is used within your organisation: this might be at faculty, departmental or course level.

It is likely that, in reflecting on your own professional practice, you define your work and your role through using 'curriculum' in more than one sense.

For example, if you are a full-time lecturer in FE teaching on a HNC unit in Sports Injuries, you might define yourself as:

- working within the sports therapy curriculum;
- teaching the sports injuries curriculum;
- working in the vocational curriculum.

Whereas if you are a part-time lecturer, teaching evening classes about the novels of Lewis Carroll and Charles Dickens, you might define yourself as:

- working within the English literature curriculum;
- teaching the Victorian literature curriculum;
- working in the adult education curriculum.

Doing more with 'curriculum'

Our second detailed example above, the vocational curriculum, is defined in part through a critical comparison with its 'counterpart' – the academic curriculum. It is in some senses easier to begin defining the vocational curriculum by thinking about what it is not. At the same time, discussions about the academic curriculum help us to frame our ideas about the vocational curriculum more carefully. These two concepts are both extremely well established. In the past there have been various attempts at creating a parity of esteem between the two in order to, so it is argued, prevent the academic curriculum from being seen as 'better' or 'superior' or 'more valuable' than the vocational curriculum. We shall return to this argument in Chapter 6. For now, it is sufficient to take note of the vocational/academic division.

The vocational/academic division is one of several such conceptual splits that are present within curriculum studies literature. Other writers and theorists have usefully added to our understanding of 'curriculum' by highlighting similar contradictions and tensions. Some of these will be discussed in the next chapter. Here, we shall focus on three such theoretical divisions, in order to extend our use and understanding of 'curriculum' within the context of the classroom or workshop. By this I mean that the issues discussed here can be conceived as being readily identifiable within a practical leaning and teaching situation, whereas those themes that are to be discussed in the following chapter are more abstract.

The planned curriculum and the received curriculum

When discussing curriculum with my teacher-training students, a frequent – and controversial – topic of conversation is the sheer amount of paperwork that awarding bodies generate. Wading through large paper documents or equally large pdf files, in order to get to grips with a new syllabus, unit or module, is not one of the most popular tasks that a tutor has to carry out. But it's unavoidable. Sometimes, tutors may receive help from colleagues, mentors or line managers in getting to know what is in the course that they are teaching. Often, however, tutors have to rely on their own experience and knowledge to make sense of course content and outlines. Adult education tutors, on the other hand, often design courses and syllabuses themselves: as such, they have much less paperwork to wade through and interpret.

At the start of the academic year (or, if you are feeling particularly well-organised, during the summer break), one of the most important jobs for a tutor to do is to draw up a scheme of work for the unit or module in question. Having read the official paperwork, the tutor has to create a week-by-week or session-by-session scheme that shows how the course will actually be delivered. Schemes of work consist of a timetable of activities, assessments and details of appropriate resources and strategies that show how the course will actually get done – what the tutors and students will actually be doing each day or week. Not all tutors have to do this: some tutors may be given a scheme of work by their line manager or course leader. Some tutors use schemes of work that are created by awarding bodies. We shall return to the mechanics of curriculum planning and sequencing in Chapter 4: at this time, it is sufficient to take note of the process.

What is happening here is that the curriculum is being relocated. It starts off in a document sent out by the awarding body, and finishes up in a scheme of work that tells the tutor who reads it how it will be delivered in a classroom or workshop. A more basic outline may also be provided for students, in a prospectus or handbook, so that they can organise their own studies and plan ahead. Such documents can be said to represent the 'planned curriculum'.

Tutors are only human, however. Some tutors find some parts of a course more interesting than others. Some will interpret some aspects of a course differently to others. Students are similarly variable in response. Some students enjoy parts of their courses more than other parts. And the need for tutors to be flexible and responsive to the needs as well as interests of their students is enshrined in policy documents, teacher training courses and QTLS standards. Bearing all this in mind, it is perhaps unsurprising to learn that two different tutors will deliver a unit or module in quite different ways, and this variation will be based on their interests and responses to the curriculum, and the responses of their students. As a result, there may be differences between what we find written down in the planned curriculum, and what takes place in the 'received curriculum' of the workshop or classroom.

Different authors use several different terms to express these ideas, although the key issue of exploring the differences or gaps between what awarding bodies and tutors plan for, and what actually happens in a classroom or workshop, stays the same.

Other related ways of thinking about the planned curriculum include:

- the official curriculum;
- the formal curriculum.

And other related ways of thinking about the received curriculum include:

- the experienced curriculum;
- the enacted curriculum.

As you might imagine, these different expressions have greater or lesser variety in the different meanings that are attached to them. 'Official' curriculum stresses the fact that in the vast majority of educational contexts, the curriculum that we and our students follow comes from, and is imposed by, a powerful, official organisation, such as a government department, a funding body or an employer-led agency. The term 'formal curriculum' invites us to imagine something called an 'informal curriculum', which tends to be defined as those things that happen outside the classroom or workshop but are still part of the official experience of an institutional education: enrichment activities or field trips, for example.

'Enacted curriculum' and 'experienced curriculum' stress the fact that the curriculum that actually exists in the classroom or workshop is something that is enacted – carried out – by tutors and students alike. The concept of the enacted curriculum allows us to make a distinction between what the official curriculum asks us to do (and assumes that we do), as teachers, and how the curriculum is actually delivered in the classroom. The experienced curriculum takes us further, by throwing a spotlight on the actual ways in which a curriculum is experienced – by students and tutors – in any one place or at any one time. This concept highlights all of those unique aspects of an educational episode: the relationship between tutor and students, the ways in which that particular group talk about or practise or disagree with what they are studying, learning or working at. Such an approach focuses on the ways in which local factors and idiosyncrasies impact on curriculum, and an analysis of curriculum using this model would suggest that every time a curriculum is delivered, it will be different.

In essence, however, they all refer to the same key issue: the gap between what it says in the curriculum documents and course handbooks, and what the tutor and students actually do.

PRACTICAL TASK PRACTICAL TASK PRACTICAL TASK PRACTICAL TASK PRACTICAL TASK

The planned curriculum and the received curriculum

How might the planned curriculum and the received curriculum actually differ? Below, we shall consider more formal ways of thinking about researching this issue. In order to begin this enquiry, think about how you might answer the following questions, focusing on one course or programme of study with which you are involved. If you are a full-time teacher-training student on a teaching placement, you may well not have had the opportunity to be involved in course design at this level, and you may wish to draw on the experience of your mentor. The questions are listed below.

1. Which parts of the course or programme do you like most, and find the most interesting and engaging? Which parts do you find the least interesting?

2. Which parts do you disagree with in some way? What is the basis for this disagreement? Do you think part of the course is irrelevant, lacking meaningful application? Do you think some of the course is out of date, or simply 'wrong' in some sense?

3. In the light of your answers to questions 1 and 2, do you think that your students notice when the course touches on those areas that you like or dislike, or agree or disagree with?

4. And which parts of the course were enjoyed or engaged with most by the students? Which parts did the students not enjoy, or find troublesome? Did you alter or modify any aspect of the course in the light of your students' responses?

The negotiated curriculum

There is one more key piece of terminology to introduce at this time: the 'negotiated curriculum'. This term is more properly used within an adult education context, and refers to the fact that in adult education, it is sometimes the case that students have some degree of control over what they will study and how they will go about it. This process is far less common than it used to be because of successive changes to the ways in which adult education classes are funded, but it does still exist. Organisations like the Workers' Educational Association, or local education authorities, still offer what used to be called recreational classes. Such classes tend to thrive on the interests and enthusiasms of the student group, who might express an interest in a particular area of study which the tutor would then deliver. Alternatively, a student group might wish to work within one aspect of a particular curriculum area. As such, the negotiated curriculum can be seen as a key aspect of adult learning theory more generally. If adult learning theory (such as andragogy, although I use the term with reservations) does indeed suggest that adults learn best when self-directed and when drawing on experience, then a negotiated curriculum would seem to be an ideal vehicle for encouraging learning, assuming that the institutional context and the awarding body allowed for such a process to take place.

This use of the term 'negotiated curriculum' is nonetheless problematic. It could be argued that meaningful negotiation is not possible because if a student group has to come to a consensus about what or how they wish to learn, then some voices will inevitably drown out others during this process of negotiation. It could also be argued that it is impossible for a student group to negotiate a curriculum in a meaningful way because they do not know enough about that curriculum to make any informed choice about what to learn or how it should be done.

The negotiated curriculum and inclusive practice

In other areas of education and training provision (mainstream FE, for example) such negotiated curricula are uncommon. That said, some aspects of official or formal curricula may be negotiable: topics for assessment, for example, may be chosen in negotiation with a course tutor; other courses may have compulsory or 'core' units and optional units that can be combined to tailor the course to suit the interests of the individual. This 'softer' negotiation can be seen as reinforcing the emphasis on inclusive learning that is at the heart of much current discussion relating to teaching in the lifelong learning sector. We shall return to this issue in Chapter 8.

Theory focus

Curriculum research

Lawrence Stenhouse, an influential educationalist and writer on the subject of the curriculum, made the gaps between the planned or official curriculum, and the received or enacted curriculum, an explicit area of research. He argued that all teachers should be encouraged to carry out small-scale research that would allow them to evaluate critically the curricula that they delivered and the impact that they had on their students. That is to say, he believed that a necessary part of the classroom practitioner's role is to study the curriculum in terms of the balance between what was intended, by the tutor, the organisation and the awarding body, and what actually happens. This approach has since been subsumed within the broader concept of *action research*:

> Action research is usually undertaken by a person who is both the researcher and practitioner/ user. For example, researchers might aim to explore how and in what ways certain aspects of their teaching are 'effective'; this research could then inform and improve their current practice.
>
> (Wellington, 2000, p194)

Talking about 'research' tends to conjure up images of scientists in white coats working in a laboratory, or of lengthy dissertations based on hours of interviews and hundreds of questionnaires. The action research approach is an attempt to encourage the kind of questioning and exploration that any research project is based on, within a teaching and learning context. For the purposes of curriculum studies, therefore, it could be argued that what is sometimes termed 'curriculum action research' is a necessary aspect of curriculum studies, assuming that any curriculum needs to be thought of, at the very least, in terms of what is planned, and what is received. Action research provides the teacher or trainer with a framework for exploring the gap between the two. We shall return to action research in Chapter 5.

Unfinished business: two definitions
Socially situated learning

Theories of learning as being socially situated assume that learning is a process that takes place as a consequence of particular kinds of human activity. This might be through observing and then modelling particular kinds or patterns of behaviour, or through taking part in particular kinds of activities. All such learning, therefore, takes place in social settings: these might be formal, institutional settings such as workplaces, or informal settings such as family homes.

Behaviourism

Behaviourist theory is best summed up as 'stimulus-response': that is to say, when a person is exposed to a particular stimulus, an appropriate response can be encouraged through offering some kind of pleasant experience as a reward. And incorrect or undesirable responses can be discouraged through offering an unpleasant experience as a reward. Such theories therefore focus on observable behaviour.

A SUMMARY OF **KEY POINTS**

In this chapter we have looked at the following key themes:

> **differing definitions of curriculum according to context;**

> **the planned curriculum and the received curriculum (and alternative ways of expressing this), and ways of thinking about the gap between the two;**

> **the negotiated curriculum, and how some aspects of specific curricula are negotiable;**

> **action research as a method of classroom or workshop enquiry.**

In the next chapter, we will add to our understanding of curriculum by looking at a number of specific concepts that have been applied to the term over the years, and these will also expand our definition of 'curriculum' (or should that be 'definitions'?). And in further chapters we will introduce some additional theoretical perspectives on curriculum relating to workplace learning as well as the learning that takes place in colleges or training centres. At this stage, the most important thing to do is to recognise the broader implications of the term, as discussed above, and to start thinking about a consistent definition that works within your own teaching or training context, that you can carry forward and modify as you work through the remainder of this book.

Branching options
Reflection

Some of the ideas that we have discussed in this chapter will be more immediately recognisable than others. The variety of professional contexts within which tutors in the lifelong learning sector work, means that although you may find that the idea of a negotiated curriculum (for example) is difficult to find in practice, a colleague or fellow-student may have an example readily available. Discuss these ideas with your peers, and discuss how useful they are (or are not) in the light of your own professional practice and requirements.

Analysis

Consider the extent to which the concepts introduced in this chapter have opened up new lines of enquiry for you, as distinct from giving names or labels to problems or dilemmas that you have encountered before. How do these conceptual tools help you to analyse the ways in which the courses on which you teach are organised and delivered?

Research

The references that appear below can be used to follow up the major themes that we have discussed in this chapter: it is not an exhaustive list, but it is manageable, and the books by Kelly and Stenhouse are particularly recommended. For those people who are interested in informal learning as distinct from formal education and training, the book by Garrick is both scholarly and readable, and as such is strongly recommended.

REFERENCES AND FURTHER READING

Garrick, J. (1998) *Informal Learning in the Workplace: Unmasking Human Resource Development.* London: Routledge.
Kelly, A.V. (2004) *The Curriculum: Theory and Practice*. London: Sage Publications.
Moon, B., Ben-Peretz, M. and Brown, S. (eds) (2000) *Routledge International Companion to Education*. London: Routledge.
Stenhouse, L. (1975) *An Introduction to Curriculum Research and Development.* London: Heinemann.
Wellington, J. (2000) *Educational Research: Contemporary Issues and Practical Approaches*. London: Continuum.

Websites

The Adult Literacy and Numeracy Core Curriculum:
www.dcsf.gov.uk/curriculum_literacy/intro/core/

A Fresh Start: Improving Literacy and Numeracy (the Moser Report):
www.lifelonglearning.co.uk/mosergroup/

The Alliance of Sector Skills Councils:
www.sscalliance.org/home/home.asp

2
Conceptualising the curriculum

By the end of this chapter you should:

- be able to evaluate critically key concepts in curriculum theory;
- know and be able to apply a range of key curriculum concepts to your own professional practice;
- understand how curriculum theory contributes to a broader knowledge and understanding of issues surrounding teaching and learning.

Professional Standards

This chapter relates to the following Professional Standards:

Professional Values:

DS 1 Planning to promote equality, support diversity and to meet the aims and learning needs of learners.

Professional Knowledge and Understanding:

BK 2.1 Principles of learning and ways to provide learning activities to meet curriculum requirements and the needs of all learners.

DK 1.1 How to plan appropriate, effective, coherent and inclusive learning programmes that promote equality and engage with diversity.

Professional Practice:

BP 2.1 Provide learning activities which meet curriculum requirements and the needs of all learners.

DP 1.1 Plan coherent and inclusive learning programmes that meet learners' needs and curriculum requirements, promote equality and engage with diversity effectively.

This chapter will allow you to work towards the following elements of the *LLUK Minimum Core*:

Language and Literacy – Personal Language Skills
Reading:

- **Find, and select from, a range of reference material and sources of information, including the internet;**
- **Identify and record the key information or messages contained within reading material using note-taking techniques.**

Introduction

Kurt Lewin, a researcher and teacher in the field of social psychology during the first half of the twentieth century, once wrote that *there is nothing as practical as a good theory*. I have always maintained that theories of learning and teaching, while sometimes holding an intrinsic interest for some, tend to be viewed in a more utilitarian manner by the majority of the students that I work with on my teacher-training programmes. This is definitely the case when it comes to curriculum theory. In this chapter, the phrase 'curriculum theory' is an umbrella term to cover all of the different ideas or concepts that are expanded upon below. Put simply, a theory is a set of ideas or concepts that are used to explain or define something. So, here, 'curriculum theory' is defined as meaning a set of ideas and concepts that can help us explain and explore what 'curriculum' actually is. On the surface, curriculum theory can seem abstract and lacking in practical applicability. In fact, curriculum theory provides the reflective student – and teacher – with a number of interesting tools with which to think about and explore the curricula within which they work. Curriculum theory can help us explain why the outcomes or objectives of a curriculum are the way that they are. It can help us provide a rationale for why some curricula actually exist in the first place. And it can help us explore those things which don't at first glance appear to be on the curriculum (or at any rate, aren't in the course documents that arrive with an increasingly heavy thud in our in-trays), but which clearly become part of the experience of following a course or programme of study for some of our students.

REFLECTIVE TASK

Defining curriculum

Before reading any further, spend a few moments thinking about how you have chosen to define curriculum as it relates to your teaching practice and experience. You may find it helpful to discuss your working definition with a peer or mentor. Go back to the previous chapter, and think again about the ideas and definitions presented there. If you didn't do so before, write up your definition of curriculum, and come back to it at the end of this chapter.

Curriculum theory: the total curriculum and the hidden curriculum

The total curriculum

In the next chapter, we will spend some time considering how curricula actually get made or formed. We will consider a number of factors to do with politics, economic and business forces, and educational perspectives, that all had an impact on shaping a curriculum which refer, in the first instance, to the actual course content: the stuff that the course or programme of study is actually about. In turn, these programmes of study find themselves aggregated into groups. So we can go from talking about the curriculum for a trowel occupations course to talking about the curriculum for the construction crafts more generally. And then we can broaden our discussions still further, to talk about the vocational curriculum. All this in some sense is to do with the curriculum, in so far as we understand that the term 'curriculum' includes what many of us refer to as the 'syllabus'.

However, the concept of the total curriculum takes us further. To understand the curriculum as a whole, in its totality, teachers and trainers need to look beyond the mere fact of what is being studied and how it is being assessed, and look to ask some more searching questions as to why a curriculum should be provided in the first place and what happens to the people who travel through it. Normally, the people involved are taken as being students, but I don't see why we shouldn't consider the impact of a curriculum on other stakeholders such as parents and guardians, employers, and even teachers and trainers. And just because a lot of the decision-making about how curricula are put together has been taken away from teachers and trainers (although there are still some exceptions, as we shall see), it is still incumbent on those same teachers and trainers – and on teacher-training students! – to think about curricula in this way. Why are these courses being run, and what will happen to our students at the end of them? What are the consequences, for all those involved, of participation in this curriculum?

Difference experiences of the curriculum

The two excerpts from learning journals that appear here contain very different sentiments about the curricula that these two trainee teachers work within. While both of them consider the curriculum in the first instance as being equivalent to a syllabus, and they work in the same area, they both broaden their scope as they write and make sense of their experience.

This is Kelly: she is employed full-time by a further education college, and teaches painting and decorating within a large prison. She is in the second year of a part-time Certificate in Education course.

> *In Cert Ed class today we were talking about the courses that we teach and about why they are done the way that they are. I'd sort of thought about this before, and some of the other members of the group couldn't believe me when I told them about my group. It all got quite cynical really and we ended up talking about politics more than education.*

> *I told them about the level 1 and level 2 painting and decorating students, because that's what I'm doing all this year. I laughed to myself when I referred to them as students, because they aren't really. Education is a big thing in the prison of course and they all have to be involved. I suppose that if they had a choice between a practical session in my workshop and a session in a classroom, they'll come to me every time. But there is often some reluctance, and it's not as if they are all going to get jobs in the painting and decorating industry once they're out. So then Dean asked me about retention and achievement, because in a college like his, the numbers are really important. But for me it's not the same. If they get released or moved, then they leave the course. And if they get released and then come back, they might join up again. For Dean, it's pretty straightforward, because all of his students are apprentices who are released to come to college by their employers. So what we ended up talking about in class was: what is my course actually for, if it isn't for turning them into painters and decorators?*

And this is Dean: he is employed by, and works in, a different further education college. He and Kelly are in the same Certificate in Education class.

Interesting teacher-training session today. Kelly was telling us about her learners. I couldn't believe it when she described her workshop facilities – they sounded absolutely fantastic. Lots of floor space, a bay for each student to work in, and more tools and kit than she actually needs at any one time. I've got nearly twice as many apprentices as she has, and I have to have them doubled up on equipment and in bays sometimes because there isn't enough space. It sounded more relaxed where she is in a way, which seems funny since she works in a prison. Then again, I've often got employers chasing around for places and wanting to make sure that their lads have completed on time. Plus my line manager is always reminding me of the need to keep progression and achievement levels high.

REFLECTIVE TASK

The painting and decorating curriculum

What sense can we make of these two quite different accounts? Both tutors are working in the painting and decorating curriculum. They both teach on accredited courses that contain formal assessment components. They both get inspected by Ofsted, and they both have to have work checked by internal and external verifiers. They are both employed as tutors by further education colleges, and they both work with similar kinds of equipment and materials. Having considered the similarities in the courses, think about the differences. Consider the places where the curriculum is offered. Think about the different students who participate in the courses. Consider how these issues are linked.

For Dean, the total curriculum can be accounted for in a fairly straightforward manner. He works with students on modern apprenticeships. They already have jobs, and need formal qualifications. This need for formal qualifications is far from straightforward, as we saw in the previous chapter. Employers want their staff to be appropriately qualified, and government departments want more people as a whole to be qualified for the workplace. Dean's job, in part, is to make sure that the apprentices are ready for the world of work, and at the same time he needs to make sure he is delivering a curriculum that reflects the needs of employers.

Kelly is delivering programmes within the same curriculum in an area that might be seen as being of economic importance: there are plenty of anecdotes about the lack of skilled craft workers such as painters and decorators, and so provision is seen as a priority. But for her, there are added complexities. She is working with students who are in prison. The idea is that armed with skills and qualifications, an ex-offender has a greater chance of economic and social rehabilitation if they are in a position to look for work on release. She might not be able to pull up a spreadsheet to prove it, but Kelly knows that most of her students will not be getting jobs as painters and decorators on release. An alarmingly high number of them may well return to prison in the future. So for Kelly, a consideration of the curriculum raises a number of issues which are not necessarily to do with a straightforward account of students gaining a vocational qualification. For her, the curriculum is about providing meaningful training and learning activities to a student group who are statistically more likely not to have any formal qualifications already. Perhaps her role is to prepare them for the possibility of further education and training upon release. Perhaps her role is to prepare them for work simply through the provision of a simulation of a working environment – a place where the students can get used to work. And perhaps her role is, quite simply, to keep them busy.

One way of explaining these differences is to return to the concept of the experienced curriculum, which was introduced in the previous chapter. This concept takes as its starting point the actual reality of the context in which a curriculum is taken part in. The two educational sites under discussion here are different in many ways, some quite profound and some with more practical consequences.

- These two student groups are very different in terms of outlook, entry behaviour and ambition. And of course, within each group, there will be considerable differences between students. Many people in the lifelong learning sector will be familiar with concepts such as differentiation and personalised learning. These ideas can help us to appreciate the fact that each student in a group will respond to the curriculum in different ways.
- The provision within these two places – a prison and a further education college – may be funded by the same organisation (the Learning and Skills Council) but that is where the similarities end. A prison culture is so different from a college culture that it is hardly surprising that both students and tutors participate – and therefore learn – differently.
- Kelly and Dean are working to very different organisational policies, reflecting the differing needs of the prison education service and mainstream further education. As such, their actions as teachers will differ. For example, pressure to maintain achievement levels can lead some tutors to 'coach' their students, adopting a surface learning approach.

A close-up look at the work done by Kelly and Dean quickly reveals two very different situations. Yes, they are following the same curriculum in so far as they are both working to schemes provided by the same awarding body and funded by the same government agency. But in almost every other way, these two educational settings are so different that we can say that the curriculum will be experienced differently in each of these places. And perhaps in many other places as well.

The hidden curriculum

Kelly's curriculum can be seen as operating at a level that does not quite match the 'official' account that might be heard from a government minister or prison governor. This is not to say that the intention to educate and thereby rehabilitate prisoners in such a way is simply an exercise in cynicism: this would be unfair to all of those involved. What is important here is that there is something else going on which is perhaps hidden from view at first sight,but which comes to the surface after some thought and reflection.

The idea of a hidden curriculum has been used by educationalists and sociologists in a variety of ways, although many of these discussions have been about what happens in schools rather than colleges or adult education centres. Essentially, definitions of the hidden curriculum tend to work in one of two ways. Firstly, there is the sense of a curriculum that contains elements that are hidden from those people who are the intended recipients of the curriculum: the students. Secondly, there is the sense of those aspects of a curriculum that are hidden from all of those involved, both students and teachers, because these elements are not consciously planned for or considered or talked about. It can be difficult to decide whether some part of a curriculum falls more neatly into one of these two definitions. What is undoubtedly the case, however, is that there is a lot more to curriculum than just subject matter and syllabus.

Theory focus

The socialising role of curriculum

Emile Durkheim, a sociologist and anthropologist of the late nineteenth and early twentieth centuries, argued that education serves as a socialising device. This can happen in a number of ways. Students can be made to feel part of a society by learning all about it: that is to say, social cohesion can be encouraged. But an educational establishment is also a society in miniature, with different social roles and responsibilities, and as such it can prepare students for the real world that is outside. The effect of the education system is to divide students according to the roles – that is to say, the jobs – they will do when they enter the world of work.

Basil Bernstein, an educationalist of the twentieth century, took a rather less benign view of the role that schools hold in preparing people for the world of work. Bernstein conceived of the curriculum as a way of restricting opportunities. Put simply, specific curricula are available to you depending on your social and economic background. As such, the curricula that you can access serve to restrict your social and economic opportunities. In this short passage from one of his books, Bernstein puts forward his conception of vocationalism. You may find it useful to return to the discussion about the vocational curriculum in the previous chapter of this book before reading on.

> *Vocationalism appears to offer the lower working class a legitimation of their pedagogic interests in a manual-based curriculum, and in so doing appears to include them as significant pedagogic subjects, yet at the same time closes off their own personal and occupational opportunities.*
>
> (Bernstein, 1990, p87)

This short quote sums up one of Bernstein's key ideas. The vocational curriculum, the courses and qualifications that are available and the ways in which policy-makers stress the value of vocational programmes and awards, in fact serve to restrict rather than widen opportunity, because they are only ever targeted at a particular sector of the population – the 'working class' – who would be doing those kinds of courses anyway.

What do you think? Discuss these theories with a colleague, or a mentor, or a fellow teacher-training student. Do the curricula within which you work *do what they say on the tin* or are there other effects that are not quite so obvious? Some issues to think about might include the following.

- Gender and race. What is the gender balance of the course, and why do you think this occurs? What is the racial mix on your course? Does your course or curriculum area make efforts to attract students from under-represented groups generally?
- Work. On vocational or occupational courses, how many students progress to working in the relevant or appropriate industry or trade sector? What happens to the others?
- Class. This might be an occasionally politically taboo topic of discussion, but it is worth thinking about. Do the courses on which you teach have distinct class identities? Are your students repeating the education and training patterns of their parents?
- Access. Are the courses on which you teach open to all? Can students with disabilities or learning difficulties come on your courses if they wish? Does the time of day or the location in which your course is run have an impact on who can attend? Is childcare available?

Not all discussions about the hidden curriculum are so controversial. For some writers, there are many aspects of curriculum that are not necessarily educationally important (examples might be the actual subject matter of the course, or embedded key skills) but are more or less important in a broader, social sense. Such issues might include the following.

- Time-keeping. The importance of punctuality and time-keeping generally might be reinforced through stressing both regular attendance at class and timely submission of assessed work.
- Personal appearance. Dress codes, including uniforms, continue to be important in many occupations. The need to maintain an appropriate appearance may be both modelled and encouraged by teachers or trainers.
- Personal conduct. Courtesy, politeness and helpfulness might seem old-fashioned virtues to some, but the potential role played by educational establishments in engendering such qualities cannot be overstated.

REFLECTIVE TASK
REFLECTIVE TASK

The hidden curriculum

Consider these three issues in the light of your own professional practice. To what extent do you model these behaviours as appropriate when working with your own students? Have you stopped and thought about these issues before? Are there any aspects of your own professional conduct that you would not wish to encourage among your students: why not?

In fact the hidden curriculum might be considered to be a powerful tool once its potential is realised. Perhaps a curriculum does not seek to reduce the life chances of the students who are exposed to it, but to enhance and expand them. Perhaps a curriculum does not simply open up new opportunities for employment to students, but opens up new social or cultural opportunities as well. A hidden agenda might have beneficial consequences. Read the following passages from Tracey's learning journal. Tracey is an adult education lecturer, delivering a range of adult and community education courses. Having completed her teacher training, she is now enrolled on a short course related to working with vulnerable adults. Here, she is reflecting on the first two sessions of a term-long course which has been designed for students with learning difficulties.

The card-making course has got off to a really good start. We have 11 students, three with support workers, and they all seem to get along okay with each other, with just one exception, but it's early days yet. I'm relieved, as preparing for the course has taken a lot of time, and only with it up and running am I going to get paid for the work I've done.

Anyway, the first two sessions have been great. All the materials and tools turned up on time for the first week so we could get straight to work. Some of the more able students have already made a card or two, and with Christmas being a couple of months away, there's a kind of added relevance or familiarity to the work we're doing, so anyone who didn't have someone they could send a birthday card to, for example, could make a Christmas card instead.

I've been really heartened by the responses of not only the students, but their support workers as well – they've given me useful feedback about how to assess the students' responses and are pleased with the level of engagement that they all seem to be showing even at this relatively early stage. And I guess that's what is important for me: not the cards as such, even though assembling the materials and planning the course took ages, but the way in which they are taking part.

Tracey's course is all about card making: that's what it says in the community education prospectus. But it's also about allowing students to take part. It could be argued that courses such as this are a legitimate form of palliative care as well as an educational experience. For

Tracey, then, discussions about a hidden curriculum might lead to a conversation about access, equality of opportunity and preventing social exclusion. Another way of considering some of these issues might be to think about her own *praxis*.

Curriculum theory: curriculum as praxis, process and product

A praxis approach to curriculum

The concept of praxis goes all the way back to Aristotle. It may be an unfamiliar word, but it is a relatively straightforward concept. Today, it means something like 'theoretically informed practice' or 'critically-informed practice'. That is to say, it is a way of thinking about what we do (our practice) as a theoretically and critically informed activity. We don't just do things in the ways that we do because we have to or because that's how our line managers want us to do them. We do things because we have a particular commitment to the action in question – in this case, to our teaching practice. This might perhaps be a philosophical or political commitment that underpins a teacher's perception of her work and role.

Praxis can be referred to in more than one way. Some uses tend to have overtly political and radical overtones. Educationalists such as Paulo Freire are referred to in this manner. Freire was a Brazilian educationalist who (among other things) argued forcefully for extensive adult literacy education and development, as an overtly political action. Other uses of praxis are to be found within the context of educational research. Critical action research (a methodology which is derived from action research, which we discussed in Chapter 1 and to which we shall return in Chapter 5) can be defined as follows:

> It has a strong commitment to participation as well as to the social analyses in the critical social science tradition that reveal the disempowerment and injustice created in industrialised societies. During recent times, critical action research has also attempted to take account of disadvantage attributable to gender and ethnicity as well as to social class, its initial point of reference.
>
> (Kemmis and McTaggart, 2005, p561)

Nonetheless, praxis is a word that gets thrown about a little too freely at times. Not everything that a teacher does necessarily counts as praxis. For Tracey, in the case study that we looked at above, a commitment to enabling access to educational opportunities among groups that have historically been excluded from education might be seen as praxis. Then again, it might simply be seen as an aspect of her broader professional commitment to her students. Tracey knows perfectly well that none of her students are going to be expert card makers by the time that their ten-week course comes to an end. For her, what is important is the taking part, not the end goal of producing the kind of handmade Christmas cards that get sold at craft fairs. Or, to put it another way, what is important is the *process*.

A process approach to curriculum

In the context of curriculum theory, a process approach is usually taken as being focused on the means rather than the ends of a programme of study. What really matters is not necessarily the end goal, the piece of paper, but the journey that the students take to get there.

Currently popular terms such as distance travelled and value added can be seen as implying a process approach to curriculum. It is the activity of learning, rather than the content of the course, that is of prime concern. The process model does not deny the importance of course content: rather, it situates it as a secondary concern. What really matters is the active role of the student in learning how to use ideas and concepts, not just information. And the teacher's role in this is to take on the role of the teacher as facilitator, with the focus being on student-centred learning.

The process model clearly has certain implications in terms of theories of teaching and learning, drawing as it does on cognitivist approaches to learning and teaching. The cognitivist school of learning stresses that learning should be seen as a process whereby students learn how to think and how to make sense of things for themselves. It is concerned more with the broader mental development of the student rather than simply meeting course objectives. And it is predicated on a model of teaching as facilitating learning, encouraging learner autonomy and self-directed learning.

The process model was developed by Lawrence Stenhouse, in his book *An Introduction to Curriculum Research and Development*, published in 1975. In it, he argued that any curriculum should have three components:

1. principles for planning a curriculum, in terms of content, teaching strategies and sequencing;
2. principles for researching a curriculum, in terms of researching and evaluating the experiences of both teachers and students, and the context within which the curriculum is delivered;
3. a justification of the curriculum which stands up to external, critical scrutiny.

Stenhouse argued that curriculum planning should focus on the gradual development of the individual student and should be shaped in large part by the teacher. Curricula should consist of guidelines and should not be overly prescriptive, and should allow for interpretation by the teacher in terms of both teaching strategies and assessment methodologies. Such an approach places a great deal of emphasis on the professional qualities of the teachers, therefore, who need to have sufficient expertise in their subject so that they can both act and react to the needs of their students. Rather than working to aims and objectives, which are seen as being overly prescriptive and lacking in genuine educational value, students should be allowed to discover and explore the subjects being studied at their own pace. In this way, Stenhouse put forward a model of curriculum planning and delivery that contrasted quite strongly with the approach that was dominant at that time, and is still dominant today: the *product* model.

A product approach to curriculum

The product model of curriculum is also known as the objectives model and is solely interested in the product of the curriculum: what can the student actually do after completing the curriculum in question? The product model is synonymous with the work of Ralph Tyler, who was an American educationalist. Tyler started out by focusing on the problem of creating assessments that could be scientifically analysed, and in his influential work of 1949, *Basic Principles of Curriculum and Instruction*, he produced a four-part model for curriculum development, the idea being that if a curriculum was specified with sufficient unambiguity and clarity, then a more scientific assessment model would follow. His model rests on four questions, which anyone developing a curriculum would need to be able to answer.

1. What are the educational purposes of the curriculum? What are its aims and objectives?
2. Which learning experiences will help these aims and objectives to be attained?
3. How should these experiences be best organised so that the curriculum is as effective as it can be?
4. How should the curriculum be evaluated? Which parts of it were not effective?

Just as the process model can be seen as resting on a cognitivist model of learning and teaching, so the product model can be seen as resting on behaviourist and/or neo-behaviourist approaches. At its heart, a curriculum should contain a concise statement of aims and outcomes, which should be unambiguous and specific. As a result of the careful specification of curriculum aims, it follows that learning activities, assessment, sequencing and evaluation will be similarly precise in scope.

The product model clearly has many attractions, not least within an educational culture that values aims and objectives models, and assessment. As such, it is not perhaps much of a surprise to learn that it can be seen as the dominant model in use in the learning and skills sector today. Even though the educational psychologies of behaviourism and neo-behaviourism are somewhat unfashionable, other aspects of these approaches to learning, such as the use of Bloom's taxonomy of educational objectives (a common feature of many teacher-training books) are still prevalent, and are perhaps not challenged as thoroughly as they might be. And from the point of view of the audit and managerial cultures within which teachers in the learning and skills sector work, such approaches are highly valued because they can be evaluated in ways which are valued by managers and government ministers: statistics, charts, and other forms of quantitative data. It is a simple exercise to evaluate an objectives-driven curriculum: they have either been met, or they have not. Evaluating the effectiveness of Tracey's card-making course would be a much more complex – and time-consuming – exercise (and we shall return to evaluation in Chapter 5).

CLOSE FOCUS **CLOSE** FOCUS **CLOSE** FOCUS **CLOSE** FOCUS **CLOSE** FOCUS

Real-life applications of the product and process models

Work through these questions on your own and then, if possible, discuss your conclusions with a colleague or a mentor or a fellow teacher-training student. Draw on your own experiences as a teacher or trainer. Look at the curriculum documents that you receive from your awarding body, as well as any other documents that you have to work with – from professional or trade bodies, for example. If you are a full-time teacher-training student, your mentor may be able to help you access these course documents if they are not readily available (for example, on the internet).

1. Go back to the four questions that underpin the Tyler model of the product curriculum. Answer them, as they relate to the curriculum within which you work.
2. Now think about any other aspects of your curriculum that you or your students experience. Do your students learn things that are not written in the course objectives, but that are nonetheless educationally worthwhile?
3. How can these other aspects best be explored? Do they constitute a process curriculum, or even a praxis curriculum?

4. Do you think that these ideas work on an either/or basis, or do you think that they all have something to contribute?

When applied to the real world, it is rare for a practitioner (or for a teacher-training student) to be able to state categorically that 'only' the process model works as a tool for analysis in their curriculum, or that 'only' the product model can explain the way that their courses are structured and assessed. Put simply, the need for our students to work towards, and complete successfully, their assessments is a key component of a product approach to curriculum. But at the same time, these students might be acquiring more independent study skills and confidence in how to apply them, a characteristic of a process model.

REFLECTIVE TASK

Redefining curriculum

Now go back to the definition of curriculum that you thought about, discussed and wrote down at the start of this chapter. Does your definition still stand, or do you feel the need to rework it in the light of what you have learned from this chapter?

A SUMMARY OF **KEY POINTS**

In this chapter we have looked at the following key themes:

> **the total curriculum: the idea that thinking about curriculum involves more than just the syllabus;**

> **the hidden curriculum: the idea that a curriculum may have unforeseen or unintended components, that may be hidden from students and perhaps from teachers as well;**

> **product, process and praxis models of curriculum: ideas about the broader educational goals being served by a curriculum.**

These themes may seem remote from the day-to-day reality of working in a busy further education college, where any time that isn't spent teaching, marking, creating resources or catching up with overdue paperwork might seem too precious to spend contemplating the hidden messages of the curriculum that you work in. And for an evening-class tutor, worrying about whether enough people will turn up to make the class viable, or even worrying about whether your teaching accommodation has been left unlocked may take up more time than considering the broader educational goals that you seek to follow. But these are valuable conceptual tools for making sense of our work and as such, deserve further reflection and application.

Branching options
Reflection

As you look back over this chapter, think about which of these ideas and concepts work for you, as well as which ones do not. Talk with people who work in the same organisation or context as you do, and then talk to people who work somewhere quite different. Compare experiences of how the curriculum works in different contexts, and consider what is valued and what is not. Is it all just about meeting the end-of-unit outcomes, or can a curriculum offer something more?

Analysis

Curriculum theory clearly has links to broader theories of learning and teaching. As professionals, we all have something of an obligation to reflect on and develop our own professional knowledge, expertise and understanding. So: how do these curriculum models contribute to your own professional knowledge? Do they complement or challenge your pre-existing ideas about learning and teaching in any way?

Research

Curriculum theory can be seen as being bound up in research almost by definition. Action research and practitioner research trace something of their ancestry back to Lawrence Stenhouse. Go back to Chapter 1 and re-read the section on action research. Look up action research and practitioner research, either in books or on the internet: how might you make use of these approaches in your own professional practice?

REFERENCES AND FURTHER READING REFERENCES AND FURTHER READING

Bernstein, B. (1990) *Class Codes and Control IV: The Structuring of Pedagogic Discourse.* London: Routledge.

Kemmis, S. and McTaggart, R. (2005) Participatory action research: communicative action and the public sphere, in Denzin, N and Lincoln, Y (eds) *The Sage Handbook of Qualitative Research*. Third edition. London: Sage.

Stenhouse, L. (1975) *An Introduction to Curriculum Research and Development.* London: Heinemann.

Tyler, R. (1949) *Basic Principles of Curriculum and Instruction*. Chicago: University of Chicago Press.

3
Shaping the curriculum

By the end of this chapter you should:

- be aware of and able to evaluate a range of theoretical perspectives relating to different social, political and economic influences on the curriculum;
- be able to begin applying these perspectives to an analysis of the curricula within which you work.

Professional Standards

This chapter relates to the following Professional Standards:

Professional Values:

AS 2 Learning, its potential to benefit people emotionally, intellectually, socially and economically, and its contribution to community sustainability.

DS 1 Planning to promote equality, support diversity and to meet the aims and learning needs of learners.

DS 2 Learner participation in the planning of learning.

Professional Knowledge and Understanding:

AK 2.2 Ways in which learning promotes the emotional, intellectual, social and economic well-being of individuals and the population as a whole.

DK 2.1 The importance of including learners in the planning process.

Professional Practice:

DP 1.1 Plan coherent and inclusive learning programmes that meet learners' needs and curriculum requirements, promote equality and engage with diversity effectively.

This chapter will allow you to work towards the following elements of the *LLUK Minimum Core:*

Language and Literacy – Personal Language Skills
Reading:

- Find, and select from, a range of reference material and sources of information, including the internet.
- Use and reflect on a range of reading strategies to interpret texts and to locate information or meaning.
- Identify and record the key information or messages contained within reading material using note-taking techniques.

Introduction

Curricula, within any formal educational context, do not simply appear out of thin air. They are created by groups of interested or appropriately qualified or experienced people. These people, and others, may well be needed to champion or defend curricula, to persuade others of their relevance or importance. This implies that these people have the authority and power to persuade others that this curriculum, in terms of what is in it and how it has been prepared, is the right one. Of course, what counts as the 'right' curriculum can and does change over time. Changing social, political and economic factors can all have an impact on the relevance, value or worth of a curriculum.

Curricula do not stand still. If we look at any particular sector of educational provision, it is easy to spot how curricula have changed over time. This can be seen as both a long-term and a short-term process. Sometimes, curricula almost disappear because the things that were being studied are no longer seen as necessary, or even desirable. The decline of the study of Latin and Greek is an example of this. A century ago, Latin was the language of scholarship, research and of the professions. Today, although Latin expressions are still used by some professions, it is no longer widely studied. Other curricula change, rather than disappear completely. The study of English literature is still very common in colleges and at universities, but the actual literature that gets studied has changed. Chaucer is no longer a staple of A level English curricula, and the study of modern fiction is much more widespread. Other curricula exist today in ways that were simply unthinkable 20 years or so ago. The rapid growth of information technologies has created both an industry and an area of study and training. At different times in the past, therefore, these different curricula have been established, maintained and sometimes altered.

Though they might seem worlds apart, thinking about Latin courses and ICT courses at the same time helps us to think about some of the reasons why curricula grow, evolve and sometimes decline. When a knowledge of Latin was necessary for some fields of employment (medicine, law, the church), it made sense for educational establishments to provide a Latin curriculum. In modern times, by comparison, the ICT curriculum has grown rapidly to service both an increasingly large industry and a society where ICT literacy is perceived as being important in the wider world of work. In this sense, a curriculum can be seen as being shaped, or driven, by the needs of employers in industry and in the professions. To put it another way, some part of the rationale for a curriculum can be found in its relevance to the world of work.

At the same time, the Latin and ICT curricula can also be seen as being driven by broader concerns that are not solely related to their usefulness in an economic sense. For centuries, the study of Latin was seen by society (or, more accurately, by a small but powerful minority in society) as being a good thing in itself. A well-rounded and well-educated person ought and needed to know Latin, and about the classical civilisation that surrounded it. Moreover, society as a whole is improved by having this knowledge and understanding perpetuated through study: the world is a better place thanks to the study and appreciation of Latin literature, poetry, history and drama. The relative scarcity of Latin in modern curricula tells us all we need to know about the cultural or social value that is attached to it today.

The prominent role of ICT within curricula today is undeniably due in part to the perceived economic benefits, whether relating to the ICT industry or to other occupations where using computers is required. Publishers, washing machine engineers and even teachers in the learning and skills sector all need to use computers at some point. But there are broader issues at work here as well, not least a sense that it is important that people 'should' know something about it. The UK government provides generous subsidies for computer classes in order to encourage people to become ICT literate. ICT can help people stay in touch with their relatives via e-mail, save money by paying gas or telephone bills online and provide a venue (through e-learning or social networking sites) for cultural activities. ICT is seen as having social and personal benefits that go beyond the purely economic.

PRACTICAL TASK PRACTICAL TASK **PRACTICAL TASK** PRACTICAL TASK **PRACTICAL TASK**

Exploring educational provision

While writing this chapter, I did a web search of courses available within my postcode area, using the www.direct.gov.uk website. My search found 726 ICT courses and six Latin courses (five of which were being offered at fee-paying schools). Many people use websites to find courses: others read through the prospectuses which are produced by local providers, in order to find a course. Have a look at the courses on offer firstly in the organisation where you work (or where you are on teaching placement, if appropriate), and secondly, where you live. Which are easy to find, and which are only available in a minority of instances? Which are subsidised and which charge a fee? If a course does charge a fee, are there concessions for retired people, or people out of work? Why do you think it is that some subjects are subsidised and others are not?

Clearly, curricula are valued and shaped by different forces. In our example we have thought about the needs of some sectors of employment, as well as broader social and cultural drivers. What this brief example also demonstrates is the value of a more detailed exploration of the things that shape the curricula within which we work. By 'shape', I mean the factors that lead to the establishment and subsequent change of curricula. In the following chapter we shall think about the actual content, the 'stuff' of a curriculum. Here, we shall focus on a number of key themes that can be said to shape or influence the curricula of the lifelong learning sector. In no particular order, since some of them do have an impact on others, these can be said to be:

- economic issues: the needs of industry, business, commerce and the professions;
- political issues: the notion of political influence on educational provision;
- social and cultural issues: the notion of an 'educated' society;
- ideological issues: the theories and beliefs that underpin formal educational provision as a whole.

As we look at these four issues, we shall think about how they affect current policy and provision within the lifelong learning sector, as well as considering some of the significant changes that have taken place over recent years. And with an understanding of these background factors in place, we shall then (in Chapter 4) be in a position better to understand which subjects, topics or skills are placed within curricula, as well as thinking about which are not.

Economic issues: the needs of industry, business, commerce and the professions

It is a commonplace that in the United Kingdom today, a significant proportion of education and training provision in the lifelong learning sector is centred around the world of work. A brief consideration of the curricula on offer at a further education college would provide us with any number of examples of courses that explicitly meet the needs of employees and employers. These include:

- plumbing;
- agriculture;
- construction;
- accountancy and book-keeping;
- sports surface management;
- electrical installation.

The relationship between the courses being studied, and the professional or vocational role that the student is preparing for, seems at first glance to be straightforward. If someone wants to be a plumber, then they can do a plumbing course. If someone wants to be a book-keeper, then there is a course for them as well. Such courses are often provided in different ways: there may be full-time and part-time options, for example (the broader topic of curriculum organisation and sequencing will be returned to in the next chapter). But such courses would be of little use if they failed to provide the appropriate or sufficient level of knowledge, ability or understanding that the student would need to be equipped with in order to gain or maintain employment. Clearly, different ways of allowing employers to have a voice in education and training are required.

Sector skills councils

A sector skills council is perhaps the most immediately recognisable employer-led organisation within the lifelong learning sector. There are 25 sector skills councils (SSCs), representing a range of industrial and commercial sectors, such as the Institute of the Motor Industry (referred to in Chapter 1), ConstructionSkills, which represents the construction industry, or skillfast-uk, which represents the fashion and textiles industry. Lifelong Learning UK is the sector skills council responsible for the development of staff working in the lifelong learning sector, and is therefore of crucial importance to anyone who reads this book!

Sector skills councils have a number of key aims which can be summarised as:

- reducing skills gaps and shortages;
- improving productivity;
- increasing opportunities for all individuals in the workforce;
- improving education and training opportunities.

The 25 SSCs are represented at a collective level by the Sector Skills Alliance, established in 2008 with an explicit commitment to the skills agenda laid out by the Leitch Report of 2007.

Professional and regulatory bodies

Many professions or occupations form incorporated bodies in order to represent and further their interests. Such bodies can be seen as a representative voice for a profession, in addition to offering educational and training guidance, accreditation and opportunities. Other occupations or trades are represented by regulatory bodies (which may also be voluntary, or have charitable status) that have a similar role in maintaining education and training standards. All such bodies may offer their own qualifications, or endorse qualifications that have been written by other awarding bodies, but following the bodies' specifications. They may draw up a document that details what they consider to be the minimum body of knowledge or skills needed for people working within the sector they represent. They may draw up more explicit guidelines in the form of National Occupational Standards. Examples of such bodies in the UK include:

- the Nursing and Midwifery Council;
- the Chartered Institute of Library and Information Professionals;
- the Association of Accounting Technicians;
- the British Computer Society;
- the National Inspection Council for Electrical Installation Contracting.

CLOSE FOCUS **CLOSE** FOCUS **CLOSE** FOCUS **CLOSE** FOCUS **CLOSE** FOCUS

Regulatory bodies in action

It may be the case that you teach or train in a curriculum area that has strong representation from one or more professional or regulatory bodies, like those listed above. Look them up on the internet, and look through any programme or course specifications that you have access to (again, these are often available online). To what extent can you trace the influence of these bodies in terms of curriculum organisation or content? What kinds of methods or procedures do they use to exert influence? If you teach or train in a context where such professional bodies are absent (for example, in community adult education, perhaps, or in an academic subject such as local history), ask the same questions about Lifelong Learning UK: think about how this SSC has shaped the teacher-training curriculum that you are currently engaged with, in terms of what the curriculum consists of, how it has to be delivered, and how it is managed.

Organisations such as those listed above are quite discrete, and tend to be readily identifiable with a particular sector of industry or commerce, or the economy more generally. All six of the curriculum areas listed at the beginning of this chapter section are directly represented by either SSCs or other professional and regulatory bodies. But there are many courses or programmes of study designed to introduce or prepare students for the world of work that take a more general approach. That is to say, while some curricula can be seen as being closely tied to specific commercial or industrial sectors, others can be seen as providing a more general education or training experience that nonetheless provides a worthwhile preparation for the world of work. So there is a distinction to be made between a specific vocational or technical education, and a broader curriculum that provides training for jobs.

The extent to which education and training should be about preparation for the world of work, as distinct from being about knowledge for knowledge's sake, has been a constant source of debate for many years, although a speech made in 1976 by James Callaghan, the then Prime Minister of Great Britain, is widely recognised as a key moment in recent history relating to the vocational curriculum.

Political issues: the notion of political influence on educational provision

In an address to the British Educational Research Association annual conference in 2007, Stephen Ball of the Institute of Education at the University of London suggested, perhaps only half-jokingly, that the reason why governments were always intervening in educational provision and practice was because they needed to be seen to be doing something, and they weren't able to make any meaningful difference in any other area of policy. Sometimes, for teachers and trainers within the lifelong learning sector, it can certainly seem that every year (if not more often) there is a new set of targets or directives from the government that lead to changes in how we work, how the courses we teach are funded or how our students are supported. Some areas of the lifelong learning curriculum seem to be more frequently affected than others: basic skills and skills for life, for example. Other policies can have an effect across the vocational curriculum as a whole. In 2006, the *Train to Gain* scheme was introduced, offering subsidised training to businesses to encourage unqualified workers to gain qualifications at National Qualifications Framework (NQF) level 2. Neatly linking these two themes, as I was writing this chapter, the UK government announced changes to the way that Basic Skills provision was to be funded through the *Train to Gain* programme.

In fact, governments have been involved in education and training policy for a long time, often (though by no means always) in response to petitions from business or industry. Rules forbidding anyone to practise a craft or trade without having first served a compulsory apprenticeship (of seven years) were originally established by government statute in 1563, and stayed in place until the Industrial Revolution when, under pressure from the new business leaders of the time, it was abolished in the early part of the nineteenth century.

During the twentieth century, the framework of the education system that we now have was gradually established. Some of these issues are fairly uncontroversial: others continue to be hotly debated. There are many places where a detailed chronology of developments in education can be found and these are listed at the end of this chapter. Nonetheless some key issues, of varying levels of controversy, are worth highlighting because of their relevance to the lifelong learning sector.

School leaving age

The school leaving age was raised to 14 in 1918, and then to 15 after World War Two. It was raised to 16 as recently as 1972. In early 2007, the UK government announced plans to raise to 18 the age at which students would have to either stay in school or be in full-time training elsewhere (in a college or workplace, for example). This change is due to come into force in 2013. This proposal has generated considerable debate. While the intention to provide appropriate education and training opportunities for everybody is laudable, reservations have been expressed. At one level, these have focused on the practicalities of the scheme. Can genuinely equivalent opportunities for all be guaranteed, irrespective of the actual place where they continue their training? And there are more profound objections as well. Are all 17-year-olds ready to continue in education? Could they not return to education later in life, when circumstances or attitudes might make for a more positive experience?

Students with disabilities

The provision of mainstream education and training opportunities for those with learning difficulties and disabilities was first established in 1970. This process was accelerated by the Education Act of 1981, three years after the publication of the *Special Educational Needs* report (the 'Warnock Report', named after Mary Warnock, who was chair of the Committee of Enquiry into the Education of Handicapped Children and Young People). In 2005, an extension to the 1995 Disability Discrimination Act made it unlawful for providers of post-16 education to discriminate against students with disabilities. To some extent, changing social attitudes towards disability have helped bring about these changes. Nonetheless, it is undoubtedly the case that legislation was necessary. Unfortunately, students with disabilities continue to face many social and institutional barriers to participation.

Key skills

Key skills is a readily identifiable term, but it still sometimes causes confusion. This is hardly surprising, bearing in mind the number of changes that 'key skills' or 'core skills' or 'transferable skills' seem to have gone through over recent years. In 1990 the National Curriculum Council published a document called *Core Skills 16–19*, which proposed the following 'core skills' to be taught across educational sectors:

1. communication;
2. problem solving;
3. personal skills;
4. numeracy;
5. information technology;
6. competence in a modern language.

In 1996, the *Review of Qualifications for 16–19 Year Olds* recommended the incorporation of three 'key skills' in A levels, GNVQs and NVQs:

1. communication;
2. application of number;
3. information technology.

The large-scale *Curriculum 2000* reforms of post-16 education included the establishment of external examinations for these three *main* key skills. The *wider* key skills – working with others, improving own learning and performance, problem solving – are not assessed by examination. The next significant change in post-16 qualifications, the new Diploma awards (although take-up of Diplomas for the 2008–9 academic year has been lower than estimated by the government), will be accompanied by a further change in key skills, which will be renamed *functional skills*. Trials of functional skills are being carried out in some further education colleges during 2008–9. They are currently defined by the Qualifications and Curriculum Authority (QCA) as follows:

> *Functional skills are practical skills in English, Information and Communication Technology (ICT) and Mathematics, that allow individuals to work confidently, effectively and independently in life.*

The constant tinkering with the system that has taken place over recent years does not tend to fill practitioners with confidence, however. At the same time, employers continue to demand more in terms of generic or transferable skills, in a manner that suggests that subsequent changes to the curriculum appear not to have been sufficiently effective.

The 'great debate'

One of the more profound recent political debates relating to post-compulsory education can be dated back to 1976, and to a speech given that year by James Callaghan, the then Prime Minister, at Ruskin College in Oxford. To supporters, Callaghan's speech was a timely critique of a curriculum that was under the excessive control of unaccountable teachers who failed to prepare people adequately for industry and commerce. To detractors, Callaghan's speech was a direct attack on the teaching profession and gave the first hint of a national curriculum that would reduce teacher autonomy and increase central governmental control.

Callaghan's speech still resonates today, as the following short extracts demonstrate. Firstly, in terms of preparing people for work:

> *...I am concerned on my journeys to find complaints from industry that new recruits from the schools sometimes do not have the basic tools to do the job that is required.*

Secondly, relating to the need for skills for industry:

> *I have been concerned to find out that many of our best trained students who have completed the higher levels of education at university or polytechnic have no desire to join industry [...] There seems to be a need for more technological bias in science teaching that will lead towards practical applications in industry rather than towards academic studies.*

Thirdly, relating to numeracy:

> *Then there is the concern about the standards of numeracy of school-leavers. Is there not a case for a professional review of the mathematics needed by industry at different levels? To what extent are these deficiencies the result of insufficient co-operation between schools and industry? Indeed, how much of the criticism about basic skills and attitudes is due to industry's own shortcomings rather than to the educational system?*

Callaghan's speech was not simply an attack on teacher autonomy. Nor was it a flawless blueprint for a national curriculum that would allow education systems to meet perfectly the needs of business and industry: Callaghan's reference to the shortcomings of industry is a sentiment that is rarely repeated by politicians today. And as for the need for a greater technological bias in science teaching, surely there is a need for both industrial application and academic study? At the heart of this debate lies not the extent to which government should or should not influence the curriculum, but the extent to which the curriculum needs to serve the political or economic needs of the country, as distinct from doing something quite different: producing a well-educated society simply because that is how society should be.

Social and cultural issues: the notion of an 'educated' society

Until the twentieth century, it was assumed that the main purpose of what was called a *liberal education* was to develop knowledgeable and cultured human beings. An education would allow a person to develop their intellectual capacities, their cultural knowledge and awareness, and their sense of responsibility and duty in the world. The liberal curriculum, therefore, is quite distinct from what might be termed the vocational, technical or professional curricula. Rather than preparing people for specific occupations or roles, the liberal curriculum was assumed to serve a more noble process: to perpetuate the culture and values of society as a whole. As such, it was seen as being more important and more worthwhile than a technical or professional education. To some extent, of course, these attitudes were bound up in broader social attitudes. A liberal education was only available to a very few, and a technical or professional education was seen as inferior because it was so closely connected to the world of work. And those other forms of education that are currently referred to as workplace learning, informal learning and family learning (to name three) simply did not feature in the debates of the time. During the twentieth century, however, as educational opportunities at all levels became more widely available, the notion of a liberal education faded in importance.

The idea that some things are important to study in their own right, because of the cultural or social importance that they hold, is still relevant today, and easily seen in the English literature or history curricula. But the narrowness of the liberal curriculum, and its focus on an education that was only available to a minority, is challenged by the fact that other curricula – vocational, technical, professional – can also be seen as contributing in a broader cultural or social sense, not just in the narrow sense of preparing people for work.

REFLECTIVE TASK

Construction courses and buildings preservation.

In this journal extract David, who is a lecturer in construction at a large FE college, reflects on meeting the parents of some of his full-time students at the start of the academic year.

Parents' evening last night. The usual mix of responses. Quite often it seems that the lads don't really want to be there and don't have too much to say. They are often more talkative when in class or the workshops. But the parents are still as mixed as ever – some very different attitudes on display. Jason's parents were always a bit hostile to the college, ever since he started. I think they never got over the fact that he didn't do as well in his GCSEs as they had wanted, so he didn't end up going to sixth form college. He's a good student, but not academic, and that's what they really wanted for him. So we were talking about the construction department generally, the kinds of work he might do when he's finished, that sort of thing. And then they asked about the other courses that we offer, so I told them about the stonemasonry courses, and the different NVQs in building conservation, and the new NVQ in Heritage Skills which started last year. And I think by the end of the conversation, their attitude had really changed. I think they had a vision of Jason working on a building site doing new-build houses or something, rather than working for the National Trust restoring ornate plasterwork or old fireplaces!

For David, the curriculum within which he works is not *just* about preparing people for work, although this is of course an important aspect of what he does. It is also about recognising that the construction curriculum as a whole is about more than building new houses. It's about recognising the value of the built environment as a whole, and the archaeological and industrial heritage that is so readily visible across the country: a heritage that needs people with the skills, knowledge and understanding of the past who can help look after them in the most appropriate and sympathetic manner.

So what, if anything, is the purpose of the vocational curriculum, or any curriculum for that matter? Simply stating that education is about preparation for employment is not sufficient, as this one example demonstrates. So perhaps there are some broader, more theoretical issues that influence educational curricula.

Ideological issues: the theories and beliefs that underpin formal educational provision as a whole

What is the purpose of education and, by extension, why are the curricula that we have shaped the way that they are? In the following chapter, we shall look in detail at how curricula are actually sequenced and delivered, and how choices about content or topics are made. But before looking at the detailed contexts in which curricula work, we need some awareness or understanding of the broader ideas or beliefs that surround them.

There are in fact many different approaches to ideologies of education in general, and curriculum in particular, and the further reading at the end of this chapter points to some of the more accessible writing on this subject. Here, we shall begin by focusing on a selection of approaches, some aspects of which have been considered earlier in this chapter, as a way of introducing broader debates about ideology and curriculum. As ever, although these categorisations are established, there is occasionally some overlap between them.

Progressive education

John Dewey, an educationalist and philosopher who died in 1952, is perhaps one of the best known, but by no means only, proponents of progressive education. For Dewey, education was bound up with broader concepts of human growth and development which last all of life. Much of Dewey's writings, as well as his real-world experience as an educator, were based on initial education. Peter Jarvis is one recent writer who has applied Dewey's approach to lifelong learning. Jarvis (2004) has argued that people have a basic need to learn, which is partly a response to living in a rapidly changing society. As a result, people need to make adjustments in order to be able to 'keep up'. Underlying any curriculum, therefore, there needs to be not only a broader concern about the development of the person, but a commitment to produce a type of person who will be a lifelong learner, able to keep pace with a changing world, and whom society needs to produce.

A commercial approach to education

In 1992, the Further and Higher Education Act was passed by parliament, and it came into force the following year. The most immediate effect of the act, within the context of the lifelong learning sector, was to release FE colleges from the control of local education authorities. FE colleges became independent corporations, businesses that would compete with each other for customers – students. The impact of what can be termed the commercialisation of further education and lifelong learning is an area of considerable debate. There is a case to be made that the overall quality of teaching that students receive has improved, and yet for some students – adult students in particular – provision has dwindled. Working conditions have also been another source of controversy and, during several years in the 1990s, were a source of industrial action. The changing role of college management has resulted in significant changes to working practices in colleges which are seen as bureaucratic and over-managed, with too much time spent on paperwork at the expense of work that is directly related to learning and teaching (Tummons 2007). Underlying the curriculum, in this sense, is a concern for the business and economic justification for its existence, rather than any sense of social amelioration or intrinsic educational worth. The curriculum is shaped by commercial and economic interests, as discussed above, and educational establishments are run as businesses.

Education as a vehicle for political and social change: humanism

The idea that education can lead to individual growth and change, above and beyond a person's ability to get a job, is a well-established one. But what if such processes of individual growth could be harnessed to a more substantial goal or project? By this I mean that if individuals can grow and change as a consequence of their education, then these individuals may well start looking at the world around them in different ways, drawing on their new learning and their new attitudes and aptitudes to critique what they see or hear or read. One of the best-known proponents of such an educational project was Paulo Freire (1921–1997), who explicitly linked the provision of adult literacy teaching with democratic renewal in South America in the early 1970s. Generally, Freire is seen as part of a humanistic tradition, due to his commitment to a democratic and truly learner-centred philosophy. However, it is important also to remember the political agenda that he followed.

Education as a vehicle for political and social change: instrumentalism and reconstructionism

Of course, political and social change is not just driven by the idealism of teachers. It can also be driven by governments and politicians. This can be seen in terms of specific workforce development to benefit the economy (an instrumental approach) or in much broader terms, as a political process that uses education as a tool. Such reconstructionist processes can be defined as being more or less benign. The negative connotations of totalitarian governments using education to control a population have to be balanced by the more positive use of reconstructionism to describe the educational philosophy of Theodore Brameld (1904–1987) for whom reconstructionist education was linked to both challenging social injustices and negotiating the aftermath of World War Two.

These themes have been chosen in order to demonstrate, in a relatively short space, that those ideas that inform decisions and opinions about what should be in curricula, and why, rest on a wide range of political and philosophical perspectives. Such ideas, more properly referred to as ideologies, often exist as pairs of opposites. And so we read about education as a way of breaking down class barriers or preserving class barriers; or as a way of preserving old knowledge or creating new knowledge. In many ways, it can be fairly argued that the lived reality of working in the lifelong learning sector leaves such arguments and issues far removed from the realities of overcrowded staffrooms, classrooms that are too small and managers who fail to respond to the needs of their teaching staff. But a sense of the broader ideas or themes that inform our working lives as tutors must surely be worth spending time on.

A SUMMARY OF **KEY POINTS**

In this chapter we have looked at the following key themes:

> the changing nature and shape of curricular provision over time;

> the economic factors that influence curriculum design, both today and in the recent past;

> the broader political factors that shape contemporary conversations about the purpose and form of the curriculum;
> the social and cultural issues that influence perceptions of curriculum;
> the importance of being aware of the ideological bases of curriculum thought.

Part of the problem with education is that almost everyone has an opinion about it: in great part, this is based on the fact that everyone has experienced it. Politicians, employers, parents and guardians, academics: all of these people (and probably others as well) help shape the curriculum to some extent, through the different kinds of pressure (more or less effective) that they can apply. For tutors, there is a responsibility to be sensitive to these pressures, not least so that we can decide for ourselves which are worth responding to, and which are worth discarding.

Branching options

Reflection

It is hard to think about these ideas and concepts when all of your time is taken up thinking about the progress that your students are making, the next class that you have to teach, or the fact that you have to stand in for an absent colleague (again!) because staffing levels are stretched. But they are important: they do shape the world in which we work. Try to take the time to consider the themes raised in this chapter and how they filter down to the day-to-day level.

Analysis

All of the issues in this chapter are worthy of a book in their own right. Some of the suggestions for further reading will allow those readers who are interested in theory to read through a more exhaustive commentary of those themes that are only briefly introduced here.

Research

As well as further reading around the ideas and concepts in this chapter, it is worth spending time reading some of the government papers and reviews that have been referred to in this chapter. They are always available on the internet and can be downloaded in pdf format so that they can be searched for particular issues or themes.

REFERENCES AND FURTHER READING REFERENCES AND FURTHER READING

Jarvis, P. (2004) *Adult Education and Lifelong Learning: theory and practice*. Third edition. London: Routledge.

Kelly, A.V. (2004) *The Curriculum: theory and practice*. Fifth edition. London: Sage Publications.

Meighan, R. and Harber, C. (2007) *A Sociology of Education*. Fifth edition. London: Continuum.

Tummons, J. (2007) *Becoming a Professional Tutor in the Lifelong Learning Sector*. Exeter: Learning Matters.

Websites

Train to Gain
http://brokers.traintogain.gov.uk/provision/qualifications/basic-skills/

The Warnock Report
http://sen.ttrb.ac.uk/ViewArticle2.aspx?ContentId=13852

The Qualifications and Curriculum Authority
www.qca.org.uk/qca_6062.aspx

4
Planning, sequencing and delivering the curriculum

By the end of this chapter you should:

- **have a critical understanding of the curriculum planning process;**
- **be able to analyse and reflect on the process of drawing up a scheme of work;**
- **understand different approaches to curriculum sequencing.**

Professional Standards

This chapter relates to the following Professional Standards:

Professional Values:

DS 1 Planning to promote equality, support diversity and to meet the aims and learning needs of learners.

Professional Knowledge and Understanding:

DK 1.1 How to plan appropriate, effective, coherent and inclusive learning programmes that promote equality and engage with diversity.

Professional Practice:

DP 1.1 Plan coherent and inclusive learning programmes that meet learners' needs and curriculum requirements, promote equality and engage with diversity effectively.

This chapter will allow you to work towards the following elements of the *LLUK Minimum Core*:

Language and Literacy – Personal Language Skills
Reading:

- **Find, and select from, a range of reference material and sources of information, including the internet.**
- **Use and reflect on a range of reading strategies to interpret texts and to locate information or meaning.**
- **Identify and record the key information or messages contained within reading material using note-taking techniques.**

Introduction

Up to this point, our studies in this book have been at quite a broad, abstract level. We have thought about defining curriculum, about how different concepts and models are applied to curriculum, and about how different external forces and agencies have an impact on what curricula actually look like. We have drawn on authentic examples and case studies to show these ideas in action, but we have yet to consider the ways in which a curriculum actually gets turned into a series of educational episodes that are accessed by students and delivered or facilitated by teachers. And so, in this chapter, we will do just that: we shall explore some different curricular requirements, and consider the ways in which teachers and trainers make decisions about how to translate a curriculum document into an actual series of sessions or workshops that will allow their students to take part in the curriculum. Or, to put it another way, we will think about how to plan and sequence a curriculum, or a component of a curriculum (a module or a unit, for example).

So what do we mean when we talk about planning, sequencing and delivering? Put simply, these terms refer to the decisions that need to be made relating to how any curriculum, or curriculum component, will actually be presented, or delivered, within an educational organisation. Choices will need to be made about how often a group of students will meet, which tutors are needed and when, and what kind of resources will be required. We will need to decide which activities to do and in what order, when assessments should be completed and in what format, and when feedback needs to be given. Before actually delivering a curriculum, there is a lot of preparation to do.

REFLECTIVE TASK

At first glance, it might appear to be the case that the task of getting a curriculum ready for delivery in the workshop or classroom would be a job for course or programme leaders or perhaps more experienced tutors. Newly appointed members of staff, whether they are on a permanent contract or even only employed on an hourly-paid basis, might think that this kind of course planning would not be part of their remit. In reality, both new and more experienced tutors, irrespective of contractual status, may find themselves involved in curriculum planning, sometimes with only a very short amount of time available before students are expecting to begin their courses! This might seem a little unfair, especially to hourly-paid tutors who might legitimately argue that course planning is 'above their pay scale', but it does happen.

As such, for those trainee teachers who are already in work and are studying part-time, course planning may well be something quite familiar. If you have been involved in curriculum planning, take a few moments to write down all of those issues that you had to plan for, such as number of teaching hours, staffing levels and resources. For trainee teachers on full-time QTLS courses, course planning will be less well known. Talk to your mentor about their experiences of course planning.

For some tutors, particularly those who work in adult and community education, curriculum planning may well involve writing the curriculum from scratch, not simply interpreting a curriculum that has already been written and endorsed by an awarding body. In cases such as these, planning the curriculum begins with actually deciding what will be in it – a freedom of action that not too many tutors enjoy these days. If you work in adult or community education and you are responsible for curriculum planning, there are two things to consider. Firstly, you need to think about how you have decided on what the course will actually be about in the first place. Secondly, you need to think about how you turn that idea into a series of sessions or lessons that will meet the needs of your students.

Schemes of work

Schemes of work, along with lesson plans, are among the most instantly recognisable pieces of paper that tutors in the lifelong learning sector have to work with. Some of the time (it may surprise you to learn) those trainee teachers with whom I work can be less than enthusiastic when it comes to writing up schemes of work and lesson plans. They are sometimes seen as a distraction from the 'real work' of teaching, and as being a paperwork burden. Now, I am not going to defend the amount of paperwork that is to be found in a further education college – or even in adult education, since the introduction of RARPA (Recognition and Recording of Progress and Achievement) – because it is considerable. However, some of the paperwork is both useful and important, and a scheme of work is one such example. The problem – if that is the right word – is that the usefulness of the scheme of work gets lost sight of amidst the broader proliferation of forms and documents. What I would like to argue for here is the completion of a scheme of work not simply as a bureaucratic exercise in quality assurance (and we shall deal with evaluation and quality assurance in the following chapter), but as a process that allows the tutor to capture, in written form, the choices and processes that have been gone through when working out how a curriculum will actually work on a day-by-day and week-by-week basis, in an authentic classroom or workshop setting. I am not saying that completing a scheme of work is all that you need to do when planning and sequencing a curriculum: there are other things to consider, as we shall see. But it does provide us with a familiar starting point as we begin to think about how a curriculum actually gets done.

Beginning the planning process: the course or programme of study

REFLECTIVE TASK

Picture the scene: there are a few weeks to go before the start of the new term, and you have just been given responsibility for a new course module. The awarding body have changed the specifications again (a process that happens quite a lot in some curriculum areas, less so in others) and so the module needs to be delivered and assessed differently from last year. What are the different factors that you need to consider when planning how the module will run?

There are three key areas to consider at this stage: course aims and content; the length and delivery pattern of the course; and teaching, learning and assessment strategies. We shall cover each of these in turn.

Course aims and content

If you are working with curriculum documents sent to you by an awarding body, then all of the information that you need relating to course aims and content will already have been supplied. Course aims are always reproduced within such documents, and tend to relate to issues such as preparing students for employment (on work-related courses such as Business and Technology Education Council courses (BTECs), for example), or for progression onto higher levels of study (on an Access to Higher Education programme, for example). At the same time, course aims may often have a broader remit as well. For example, English for Speakers of Other Languages (ESOL) courses, while understandably stressing the fact that improving your spoken and written English can help you find employment, also highlight the broader social and cultural benefits that improving your English can bring, such as social integration, or access to other public services.

Course aims, of whatever kind, can be seen as directly impacting on the student and on the learning journey that they are about to undertake. As such, it is important that there is some consideration of the needs of the student. To that end, curriculum documents invariably include details relating to expected student entry behaviour, such as prior qualifications or work experience. For example, it is common practice for a course at NQF level 3 to state that an applicant would have to be already qualified at level 2, in a relevant subject, before being admitted to the course. Course documents may also contain information about procedures that should be followed if a student with special educational needs (SEN) wished to enrol on the programme, although sometimes the tutor will be directed to a separate document. There may also be guidelines as to the number of students that can be in a class at any one time, although this might also depend on the actual accommodation available at an institution.

Course content will also be indicated by the awarding body's curricular documents. An outline syllabus will provide details of the key issues, topics or competences that need to be covered during the course in question. Other information may also be included, such as recommended reading lists, recommended assessment strategies, or mandatory learning and teaching activities. The syllabus may also be cross-referenced to appropriate national occupational standards, the code of practice of a professional body, or a broader initiative such as *Every Child Matters* or key skills. (Key skills were discussed in the previous chapter, and we shall return to *Every Child Matters* in Chapter 8.)

Other kinds of information may be included as well, although different awarding bodies and examination boards have different ways of doing things. Among the other procedures or pieces of information that might be found are: details relating to internal moderation; external examination or validation procedures; and what to do in the case of complaints or grievances.

Course length and delivery pattern

The amount of time that a course requires tends to be specified in a number of ways, although these normally relate to guided learning hours, and these in turn are often linked to funding. That is to say, providers are funded (usually by the Learning and Skills Council) to deliver courses in part according to the amount of time that the course requires in order that it can be correctly delivered. (Other aspects of course funding relate to retention and achievement rates.) But some flexibility is to be found in this approach. The week-by-week scheduling of a course that is described as requiring a specified number of guided learning hours could vary between institutions should local circumstances require it.

CLOSE FOCUS **CLOSE** FOCUS **CLOSE** FOCUS **CLOSE** FOCUS **CLOSE** FOCUS

Defining guided learning hours

Quite specific criteria are attached to guided learning hours. The Learning and Skills Council defines them as follows:

1. Guided learning hours are defined as all times when a member of staff is present to give specific guidance towards the learning aim being studied on a programme.
2. Guided learning hours include lectures, tutorials and supervised study in, for example, open learning centres and learning workshops.

3. It also includes time spent by staff assessing a learner's achievements, for example in the assessment of competence for National Vocational Qualifications (NVQs).

4. It does not include time spent by staff in the day-to-day marking of assignments and homework where the learner is not present, nor does it include hours where supervision is of a general nature and is not specific to the study of learners.

A simple example of this might be the choice of whether to deliver a course requiring 48 guided learning hours over 16 weeks, with three hours allocated for each session, or over 12 weeks, requiring four hours for each session. There are several factors that contribute to decisions such as this. At a practical level, the kinds of things that need to be considered are term dates (and the timing of public holidays, for example), room availability, timetabling and staff availability. Even time of day makes a difference: the decision to arrange a four-hour class during the daytime would be perfectly straightforward. A four-hour evening class would cause potential students more problems: the class would have to start when some of the students might still be at work, or collecting children. From personal experience, I know that teaching a three-hour evening class to a group of students who have just done a day's work is sometimes challenging: I am not sure I would want to teach them for an extra 60 minutes. Nor do I think it would be in the best interests of the students to ask them to take on a class of this length at the end of the working day.

Exact details over timetabling and class length and number therefore depend in part on the entry profile of the students. Similar awards or qualifications might be delivered using a very different pattern or sequence, depending on the needs of the students. Students who are in employment, and who rely on the mutual co-operation of their employers and the college that they hope to attend, may find themselves attending college at different times. For example, a further education college might offer a level 2 Intermediate Construction Award In Trowel Occupations on a day-release basis, with students attending college for one day a week, or on a block-release basis, when students would attend college for a week at a time, for a total of 16 weeks during the year as a whole.

There may be other practical issues that have an impact on exactly when and where particular curriculum units or modules are delivered. The availability of suitable accommodation, or suitable staff, might mean that particular units have to be run at specific times during the academic year. The size of a student cohort may be restricted by the availability of classroom or workshop resources. The lack of suitably qualified staff may mean that the delivery of a particular course component might have to be delayed or even cancelled. Some qualifications consist of both compulsory (core) and optional units, and the choice of which optional units to offer students may similarly be constrained by the availability of suitably qualified and experienced staff, or of appropriately equipped teaching accommodation. We shall return to the issue of staff expertise shortly.

Teaching, learning and assessment strategies

As with those issues already discussed, teaching, learning and assessment strategies are also often to be found within the documentation sent out by awarding bodies. Again, the level of detail provided will depend on the awarding body in question. Some bodies offer only bare outlines that then have to be filled out by tutors; others provide quite detailed specifications that have to be carefully followed (and the extent to which procedures are followed will be checked up on by external verifiers, as discussed in the following chapter).

Sometimes the guidance given will include ideas for specific strategies, such as using case studies or simulations, or planning activities that will require students to practice particular skills, such as using an Excel spreadsheet. At other times, broader themes and issues are stressed, such as the need to ensure that appropriate links to current workplace practices are included by teaching teams when delivering a programme.

CASE STUDY
Delivery and assessment strategies, and resources

The BTEC National Diploma in Electrical/Electronic Engineering is a modular work-related qualification. Unit one of the award, *Business Systems for Technicians*, is detailed using a standard format that includes recommendations for delivery strategies, assessment strategies and resources.

The recommended delivery strategies include:

1. case studies based on either real or fictional companies;
2. small group work;
3. visits from industry personnel;
4. using real or fictional datasets to create Excel spreadsheets.

The assessment strategies include:

1. portfolio building advice, including what to include – assignments, case study work, course notes and work done during class;
2. a requirement to map portfolio evidence onto unit learning outcomes.

The recommended resources include:

1. internet and ICT access;
2. textbooks;
3. legislation.

For experienced tutors, this level of information might seem to be unnecessary, perhaps even patronising. But it is important to remember that new tutors are joining the workforce in the learning and skills sector all the time, and that while new tutors will have appropriate qualifications and experience in their subject area, they will rarely come into education with a teaching qualification. Certainly, some of the trainee teachers that I have worked with have expressed gratitude for such a detailed level of advice and guidance from awarding bodies.

Beginning the planning process: the role of the tutor

We have already hinted at the need for suitably experienced and qualified staff in order to ensure the smooth running of a curriculum. Even if the rooms are well equipped and spacious, the photocopies are clear and legible and the timetabling means that the course is running at the most convenient time imaginable, if the teaching and training staff lack sufficient authentic expertise – whether this derives from industrial experience, professional or trade qualifications or a combination of the two – then the delivery of the curriculum will suffer. It is quite understandable, therefore, for awarding bodies to stipulate the qualifications and/or experience that they would wish those teachers working on their programmes to possess. Or, to put it another way, teachers and trainers need to have appropriate and current vocational or professional qualifications. At the same time, the lifelong learning sector as a whole is understandably concerned to ensure that students receive a sound educational experience, and one of the measures taken to ensure this is to work towards a qualified teaching workforce. Or, to put it another way, teachers and trainers need to have appropriate teaching qualifications.

So what are those areas of professional or vocational expertise that a tutor needs to have? There are two ways to consider this question: in terms of knowledge and experience of the specialist area or subject in question; and the ability to plan for and use appropriate learning, teaching and assessment strategies.

Knowledge and experience of the specialist area

It might seem obvious to state that a teacher or trainer needs to know the subject before they teach it, but this is not always the case. Sometimes it may well be difficult for a college or adult education centre to find appropriately qualified staff, which is why 'golden hello' payments were introduced to attract new staff to the sector. Sometimes, however, we may find ourselves teaching within a curriculum area that we are not entirely fluent or comfortable in. Ideas about a 'flexible' workforce are widespread in many sectors of business and industry and the need to be 'flexible' in such a manner is quite typical of the learning and skills sector generally, and the mainstream FE sector specifically, and tends to be portrayed as a positive and desirable quality by college corporations and senior management teams.

Undoubtedly there are benefits to such an approach. Working within and across different curriculum areas can be helpful and illuminating for teaching staff, who may well gain valuable professional experience from such a mixture of experiences. However, a focus on flexibility can come at the expense of technical or vocational specialism and expertise, and this can be seen as having a damaging effect on the professional status of the individual tutor (Shain and Gleeson, 1999). In this sense, a flexible workforce leads to a de-skilled workforce, with specialist tutors replaced by generalists who can be slotted in wherever a tutor is needed, in a manner typical of a 'make do and mend' ethos. But at the end of the day, there can surely be no disagreement over the fact that students deserve and need qualified and knowledgeable teachers and trainers. Such knowledge will usually rest on two foundations: relevant and up-to-date qualifications; and broader experience.

Appropriate qualifications are of course absolutely necessary for any teacher or trainer in the lifelong learning sector. But so too is appropriate experience, generally in terms of previous employment, or practical experience. The desirability of experience, together with qualifications, is clearly beneficial to students, who will be able to relate to and learn from the authentic experience that their tutors bring with them. In this way, having an experienced tutor can be seen as encouraging successful learning. As such, it is clearly beneficial for tutors to engage in continuing professional development (CPD) and to update not only their knowledge of learning and teaching (through the recently introduced CPD programme that is managed by the Institute for Learning) but also their specialist area knowledge and understanding. Indeed, some professional bodies already stipulate that members need to undertake CPD on an annual basis (Tummons, 2007). In a similar spirit, the qualifications and CPD records of delivery teams are often evaluated by external verifiers or inspectors.

Planning for and using appropriate strategies

It is one thing to know your subject: it's quite another to be able to communicate it effectively to a group of students. (We shall consider the theories that lie behind this statement in Chapter 6.) This, of course, is why teachers and trainers have to do their QTLS courses. Indeed, the differences between knowing about something and being able to teach it seem to be so obvious that it is surprising to learn that compulsory professional teaching qualifications – awards that now lead to QTLS – have only been around for the last decade or so. Not that a qualification in teaching necessarily means that the award holder is automatically going to be a good teacher, but the odds are improved.

When considering the staffing requirements of a particular curriculum, the demands placed on the teaching team can be seen as being more specific than a generic teaching qualification can allow. Teacher-training programmes can and do help students to learn about pedagogy – about learning, teaching and assessment. Nevertheless, the sheer diversity of the curriculum in the lifelong learning sector more generally makes it very hard for any one of those curricula to be explored, from the point of view of pedagogy, in great depth. This is hardly surprising at even a practical level: we can consider the mix of sectors and curriculum areas that a typical teacher-training group might come from.

CLOSE FOCUS CLOSE FOCUS **CLOSE** FOCUS CLOSE FOCUS **CLOSE** FOCUS

A mixed teacher-training group

Spend a few moments writing down all of the different curricular areas that your fellow students come from. The CertEd/PGCE group that I am working with this year represents the following sectors:

- basic and key skills;
- beauty therapy;
- business studies;
- childcare studies;
- ESOL;
- hairdressing;

- health and safety;
- ICT;
- life skills;
- management;
- manual handling;
- music.

And a similarly diverse group of employment contexts is also present. The teachers and trainers in this group work in:

- family learning centres;
- further education colleges;
- community education centres;

- prisons;
- hospitals;
- private companies.

Diverse teacher-training groups are far from uncommon in the learning and skills sector, and although some programmes of study within the post-compulsory education and training (PCET) curriculum do make provision for developing subject-specialist pedagogies (although this is all too frequently limited to mentoring), most programmes are generic.

What does all this have to do with planning for and using appropriate strategies? There are a few themes to consider in response to this question. Firstly, while teaching qualifications do have value, it is important to consider the broader educational experience of any teacher or trainer in the context of the curriculum that they are being asked to teach. The specific demands of any curriculum might be expressed in terms of content (that is to say, a particular specialist body of knowledge or of competences), or of particular requirements for teaching activities (that is to say, the use of specific ICT applications, or specific pieces of machinery). Sometimes such demands are implicit, and only a very careful study of the curriculum documents that have been sent out by the awarding body will bring them to light. At other times, those same documents might set out specified criteria for particular activities or resources that must be used for curriculum delivery.

CLOSE FOCUS **CLOSE** FOCUS **CLOSE** FOCUS **CLOSE** FOCUS **CLOSE** FOCUS

Case studies in curriculum delivery

It's time now to think in broad terms about the things that we have covered in this chapter up to this point. Read through the following three case studies, each of which provides brief details relating to tutors working in the lifelong learning sector. As you read, think about how you might answer the following question in relation to each case study: to what extent has the delivery of the curriculum been effectively planned to meet the needs of the students, and what challenges might arise as the curriculum is delivered?

CASE STUDY
Sarah

Sarah teaches just two adult education classes each week. She has been working in adult education for several years. She teaches textiles and home furnishing courses to adults who attend evening classes lasting two hours. This provision is organised by the local education authority where Sarah lives. The classes are held in a local secondary school, which provides accommodation for several adult education classes during term time evenings. In order to become financially viable, the textile courses are accredited: one through RARPA (Recognition and Recording of Progress and Achievement), and the other through Open College Network accreditation. As such, students do complete portfolio-based assessments during their time on the courses. Sarah has a large number of relevant professional and craft-based qualifications, as well as varied commercial experience in textiles and home furnishing. She has recently completed her PTLLS award (Preparing to Teach in the Lifelong Learning Sector).

CASE STUDY
Tom

Tom is a tutor in plumbing, working at a mixed FE college. He works on an Advanced Apprenticeship programme, leading to the award of a level 3 NVQ. The programme is open only to students who are already employed by a plumbing firm. Students attend college on a day-release basis. At the moment, there are two student cohorts: one group attends college on a Tuesday; the other on a Friday. The plumbing workshop at the college is relatively small, whereas student groups are sometimes quite large. Tom is currently halfway through his Certificate in Education programme, leading to QTLS. He is a qualified plumber and has several years' industrial and commercial experience. He works full-time at the college, although he still works as a plumber, now on a self-employed basis, at weekend.

CASE STUDY
Shazia

Shazia is a Skills for Life ESOL tutor, working at a family learning centre, although employed by the local FE college. The ESOL programme that she works on is free, and is targeted at those groups of students who are described as hard to reach and vulnerable (as distinct from work-based ESOL courses). She teaches for two mornings a week, from 10 a.m. until 1 p.m. She is in her third year of ESOL teaching: this has been her first teaching role. Although she is employed on an hourly-paid basis, working as a teacher is her main form of paid employment. Upon entering her third year as a teacher, she has now chosen to undertake a Certificate in Education course. She already holds a Certificate in Adult ESOL Subject Support.

Case studies: responses

A number of issues arise from these case studies. Some of the things you might have thought about include the following:

- Accommodation. For Shazia and Tom this isn't much of an issue, although Tom may find the workshop getting a little crowded from time to time, and so he will have to be careful about the exact order in which he plans his sessions to prevent too much of a squeeze. Sarah has more profound problems in this regard: evening class tutors end up in all sorts of places (primary school classrooms, sports pavilions, village halls) and facilities tend to be scarce.
- Resources. Sarah may well have concerns here as well, as she will have to bring everything she needs with her, and then take it away again after the end of her two-hour class. Packing and unpacking rolls of wallpaper, boxes of fabric swatches and photographs of house interiors all takes time.
- Qualifications and experience. Shazia's qualifications raise some concerns. Strictly speaking, her level 3 certificate is a qualification for learning support, not for teaching. A level 3 qualification is perfectly acceptable as an entry qualification for a teacher-training programme, but she also needs to be aware of the need to obtain a level 5 Additional Diploma in Teaching English (ESOL) if she wants to be fully qualified as an ESOL teacher.

Of course, there are other issues to focus on as well: the impact of assessment – both positive and negative – on what is essentially a recreational programme (Sarah); or the benefits of being able to bring experience into the classroom (all three of our tutors, in their own ways). What is important is that the implications for how a curriculum might be delivered and experienced can be critically analysed – in part – through consideration of the resources, accommodation and staff who will deliver it. And a consideration of these issues is a necessary part of the planning process.

The planning process: getting things in order

There is one last issue to consider, and this is possibly the most important issue to be considered in this chapter up to now: the exact order in which different subjects or units should be arranged when planning a sequence of lessons. There are several important theoretical approaches to this, which are dealt with in detail in Chapter 6. Here, it is sufficient to acknowledge that the specialist knowledge or ability of a tutor needs to be presented to students in such a way that learning can take place. Normally, this requires the different areas or topics of a course to be introduced and then followed in a particular sequence. Such a sequence assumes that subjects or skills are introduced according to two overlapping principles: the level of difficulty of the skill or task; and the extent to which a skill or task relies on the prior understanding or mastery of another curriculum component.

It stands to reason that students would find it difficult to attempt complex tasks before being able to master more straightforward ones. Asking a trainee electrician to wire up a lightning conductor would be an unfair request if that trainee had yet to be shown how to strip and route electrical cables properly. Asking a student on a European Computer Driving Licence (ECDL) course to attach a Word document to an e-mail which then needed to be sent to multiple recipients would prove difficult if that student had not yet been shown how to set up an e-mail account.

So, when planning how a curriculum should be delivered on a session-by-session basis, the first priority should be to consider what order the different parts of the course should be put in, in order that students have the maximum opportunity for understanding and learning.

Back to schemes of work

At this time we can summarise the issues that we have to consider, when planning and organising our curriculum, as follows:

- course aims and course content;
- course length and delivery pattern;
- an appropriate order in which areas or subjects will be covered;
- learning and teaching strategies;
- assessment;
- the specialist knowledge and experience required.

Now we are in a position to consider carefully and critically the generation of a scheme of work. It is common practice for larger, more complex institutions such as further education colleges to provide a standard template for each scheme of work that is required, simply because a standardised approach makes things a bit easier from the point of view of quality assurance. Such an approach clearly has merit, although from time to time practitioners may find the regime of box-filling a bit difficult to do in a meaningful way. I have seen schemes of work that include a column for tracking coverage of *Every Child Matters*: useful if working with a 14–16 or a 16–19 group, but perhaps less so on a higher education course for adults. Some schemes of work ask tutors to track key skills; others have a column to show coverage of different learning styles (something that I have a bit of a problem with, I must admit). Tutors in less formal institutional settings – community education, for example – may also find themselves asked to use a template if they are working on an accredited programme.

Examples of blank lesson plans appear in several QTLS textbooks and I do not propose to produce another one here, partly for that reason, and partly because it is more than likely that a teacher or trainer will need to use a scheme of work based on a template that has been created within their organisation. For those who do wish to browse some alternatives, a good place to start is the collection of teaching and learning resources at the Quality Improvement Agency (QIA) Excellence Gateway. (It is worth noting that the QIA has now been subsumed into a new organisation, the Learning and Skills Improvement Service.)

The planning process: who is it for?

This might seem like a curious question. Surely the answer must be that the planning process is for the benefit of the student, because it shows that the tutor has spent time thinking about how best to deliver the curriculum. In fact, things aren't quite that simple. The world of inspection and audit in which we, as teachers and trainers in the lifelong learning sector, now belong requires that all aspects of our professional work come under scrutiny. Inspectors, line managers and external verifiers, to name three, all require proof from time to time that we are doing our jobs according to the appropriate criteria. As such, a scheme of work, and any other appropriate documents (tracking sheets, tutorial records, feedback sheets and the like) becomes an object for evaluation (discussed in more detail in the following chapter). Here, it is sufficient to note that the planning process is not solely for the student's benefit, or even for the tutor's. Planning processes are also aimed, in part, at Ofsted inspectors and external examiners. They are not only for students, but also for line managers, management information systems (MIS) officers and course leaders. Indeed, it could be argued that because schemes of work tend to be detailed, bureaucratic documents, they are not really suitable for giving out to students at all, and perhaps a very different style of document is needed to provide students with an outline of the course or programme that they are undertaking.

Sequencing models: linear, spiral and thematic curricula

Finally, we are in a position to think about some different theoretical approaches to the ways in which curricula as a whole are organised or sequenced. There are essentially three ways of thinking about curriculum sequencing, although in reality it is quite possible for any single curriculum to have aspects of more than one of these models present within the overall scheme. The three curriculum sequencing models are: linear sequencing; spiral sequencing; and thematic sequencing.

Linear sequencing

In a linear curriculum sequence, the different areas or topics that make up the curriculum as a whole are arranged one at a time according to the requirements of the programme. Typically, that might involve arranging curriculum units according to levels of difficulty, or increasing complexity. Once the module or unit has been run – that is to say, once the module has been taught, assessed and the results of the assessment recorded – then it is completed and there is no formal need to return to it. In a linear sequence, modules are treated on a standalone basis with no formal integration. A standalone PTLLS course provides a good example of a linear sequence.

Spiral sequencing

In a spiral curriculum sequence, the different areas or topics that make up the curriculum are studied more than once. At first, they are covered at a relatively brief level, and then they are returned to so that they can be explored more critically, usually over a longer period of time. A spiral sequence therefore allows students more quickly to gain an overall sense or picture of the course being undertaken, thereby allowing them to learn in a more holistic manner, although there is a consequent risk that a spiral sequence can be seen as repetitive. A CertEd/PGCE course with an embedded PTLLS component provides a good example of a spiral sequence, with the subjects that make up the PTLLS component returned to in much greater detail during the rest of the course.

Thematic sequencing

In a thematic sequence, some of the different units that made up the curriculum would include core or key themes that would be returned to throughout the course as a whole. These central themes would be seen as underpinning all of the work that students do while studying the curriculum. Other themes or topics would be introduced, practised or studied and then progressed from as the course ran. The way that reflective practice is embedded across the QTLS curriculum provides a good example of a thematic sequence.

REFLECTIVE TASK

Curriculum sequencing

Choose one particular curriculum within which you work, and apply the linear, spiral and thematic sequencing models to it. To what extent are different aspects of your curriculum satisfactorily analysed through the use of these ideas? If you are currently working towards QTLS or PTLLS, to what extent do you think this curriculum follows one or more of these models?

A SUMMARY OF **KEY POINTS**

In this chapter we have looked at the following key themes:

> **key issues in planning and sequencing a curriculum: course aims and content; learning and teaching strategies; assessment; course length and delivery pattern;**

> **drawing up a scheme of work, and the different purposes that a scheme of work fulfils;**

> **theoretical approaches to curriculum planning: linear, spiral and thematic sequencing.**

Deciding the running order for a course or programme of study takes longer to get right than you might think although, over time, the professional expertise that you acquire helps these decisions come more quickly and fluently. Nonetheless, careful thinking about both how a curriculum should actually be run and what resources (in the broadest sense of the word) are needed is essential if we want to make the most of the opportunities for learning that the students will be exposed to.

Branching options

Reflection

It is easy to over-theorise some aspects of curriculum studies, and to lose sight of the practical issues among the welter of theories and models that is to be found in textbooks. Nonetheless, drawing up schemes and sequences for a curriculum is a process that requires and deserves critical reflection, even though it often feels like 'just another paperwork exercise'.

Analysis

It should not be difficult to find multiple examples of schemes of work that are currently being followed within the institution that you teach in (or that you are in during a teaching placement). Select two or three schemes of work (from different curricular areas, if possible) and unpack them: think about the assumptions – in terms of running order, resources, assessment timings – that were made when the scheme was written up, and evaluate these decisions.

Research

One fruitful area of further research is the link between curriculum sequence models and learning theories. The obvious link to draw is that between a spiral model and a cognitivist learning theory (hardly surprising, given the role of Jerome Bruner in researching and theorising both of these). One question that might be worth asking is: to what extent do the sequencing models represented here assume or promote one model of learning over another? The references below will provide a starting point for more in-depth research.

REFERENCES AND FURTHER READING

Cornford, I. (1997) Ensuring effective learning from modular courses. *Journal of Vocational Education and Training,* 49(2): 237–251.

Neary, M. (2002) *Curriculum Studies in Post-compulsory and Adult Education.* Cheltenham: NelsonThornes.

Shain, F. and Gleeson, D. (1999) Under new management: changing conceptions of teacher professionalism and policy in the further education sector. *Journal of Education Policy,* 14(4): 445–462.

Tummons, J. (2007) *Becoming a Professional Tutor in the Lifelong Learning Sector.* Exeter: Learning Matters.

Websites

The LSC definition of Guided Learning Hours can be found at:
www.lsc.gov.uk/providers/Data/datadictionary/businessdefinitions/GLH.htm

For information about 'golden hellos' for FE teachers:
www.teachernet.gov.uk/professionaldevelopment/careers/post16/fegoldenhellos/

The Learning and Skills Improvement Service website is at:
www.lsis.org.uk/LSISHome.aspx

5
Evaluating the curriculum

By the end of this chapter you should:

- have an understanding of evaluation methods, scope and rationale;
- be able to discuss the roles of different stakeholders in the evaluation process;
- have an awareness of some of the debates that surround evaluation in the lifelong learning sector.

Professional Standards

This chapter relates to the following Professional Standards:

Professional Values:

AS 5 The importance of reflecting on and evaluating own practice as teachers, tutors or trainers against the value base of QTLS.

ES5 Working with the systems and quality requirements of the organisation in relation to assessment and monitoring of learner progress.

Professional Knowledge and Understanding:

AK 5.1 The impact of own practice on individuals and their learning.

EK 5.1 The role of assessment and associated organisational procedures in relation to the quality cycle.

Professional Practice:

AP 5.1 Reflect on and demonstrate commitment to improvement of own teaching skills through regular evaluation and use of feedback.

EP 5.1 Contribute to the organisation's quality cycle by producing accurate and standardised assessment information, and keeping appropriate records of assessment decisions and learners' progress.

This chapter will allow you to work towards the following elements of the *LLUK Minimum Core*:

Language and Literacy – Personal Language Skills
Reading:

- Find, and select from, a range of reference material and sources of information, including the internet.
- Use and reflect on a range of reading strategies to interpret texts and to locate information or meaning.
- Identify and record the key information or messages contained within reading material using note-taking techniques.

Introduction

Handing out and collecting end of term questionnaires from students is sometimes a monotonous task. In some of the places where I have worked, questionnaires have been handed out so often that some of the students start to begrudge filling them in, a phenomenon that I call questionnaire fatigue. Students complete them in a rather cursory fashion, often not even reading the instructions properly, and seem to give little heed to what will happen next to the completed forms. And in a way this is a pity, because completing end of term or end of course questionnaires such as these constitutes one of the most common and easily visible aspects of the quality assurance systems that are present throughout the lifelong learning sector. End of term questionnaires are a simple evaluation tool, admittedly, but they perhaps need to be taken more seriously than is sometimes the case. If we accept that the courses and curricula that we work on are to be evaluated, then it follows that we need to explore critically both the ways in which and the reasons why such evaluations take place. To begin with, however, we need to establish a working definition of curriculum evaluation.

REFLECTIVE TASK

Before reading on, spend a few moments considering how you might define evaluation within the curricular context in which you work. Discuss your definition with a fellow student, or with your mentor.

Now go on to think about the kinds of ways in which those curricula that you are or have been involved in have been evaluated.

Defining evaluation

I often ask my own teacher-training students to consider definitions of evaluation, and some typical responses to the question 'What is evaluation?' have included:

- finding out if your course or curriculum did what it set out to do;
- judging fitness for purpose;
- making sure the curriculum is value for money;
- seeing if all of the resources that you use are of an appropriate standard;
- making sure that the students have got from the course what they expected to get, and what everyone else expected that they'd get;
- keeping the government happy.

These sorts of issues are a good place to start, not least because they provide an indication not only of what curriculum evaluation is, but also of the different people, or stakeholders, who are involved in the process at some point. So, to begin, we can define evaluation as a process, or a number of processes, by which we can find out how well a course or curriculum is running, from the point of view of all those people who have a legitimate interest in it. In order to carry out an evaluation we need to gather and then analyse a body of relevant information that can help us respond to the kinds of issues highlighted above.

Evaluation is not a straightforward process, however: there are disagreements about evaluation at both theoretical and practical levels. Theoretical disagreements include questions relating to the kinds of data that need to be collected, and which kinds of data can produce a valid and reliable evaluation. Practical concerns relate to the time and resources that evaluation procedures seem to require, and the – at times – stressful impact of some of the more onerous forms of evaluation (Ofsted inspections being a good case in point). Before exploring these more complex issues, however, it is necessary to think in detail about exactly what we are evaluating and who the different stakeholders in the process actually are.

> ## REFLECTIVE TASK
>
> Before reading on, return to Chapters 1 and 2 and revisit the different definitions and models of curriculum that were explored there. A coherent approach to any evaluation of the curriculum will depend in part on what you think the curriculum actually is and what it is supposed to do. As we shall see, differing definitions of curriculum work alongside differing models of evaluation. For the first reflective task in this chapter, you will have spent time thinking about those evaluation methods and principles that are relevant to your own professional practice. As you read on, think about these evaluation methods and the kinds of curriculum concepts that they rest on.

What should we evaluate?

If the purpose of evaluation is to find out how well a curriculum is performing or being managed or being delivered, then we need to evaluate any thing or person or institution that is involved in the delivery of that curriculum. So, to some extent, the scope of our evaluation will be defined by the ways in which the curriculum is viewed.

So, what might we evaluate?

Material resources

At a practical level, we have to consider the effectiveness of all of the materials, resources and people that are required to deliver a curriculum successfully. Trying to teach a City and Guilds Bricklaying course without appropriate tools and materials would quickly lead to problems. Courses such as these need properly qualified teachers (that is to say, with appropriate and current trade and industry qualifications in addition to a teaching qualification, or a commitment to obtain one). They also need sufficiently large workshops, a ready supply of materials, proper equipment and sufficient allocations of time. This is not the same as saying that courses always need to have plentiful supplies of cutting-edge equipment. Tutors working on courses in community outreach settings often have to make do with equipment or facilities that are of a lesser quality than they might be able to draw on if working at their home institution. Some parts of the lifelong learning sector are funded at quite modest levels, and buying expensive computer equipment is simply unfeasible. But even if a tutor only has an old projector and some handouts, rather than a brand new laptop and data projector, the resources still need to be as good as they can possibly be.

Successes and failures

From the point of view of a product model of curriculum, we have to consider the success or failure rates of those students or trainees who have been through the curriculum. If a significant number of students on a Skills for Life course that is being run at a particular centre are dropping out before the course ends, or are failing to achieve, then there may be a problem of some kind at an institutional level. If these problems are repeated across multiple sites, then there may be a more profound problem with the way that the course has been put together, rather than simply with how it is being delivered. At one level, the success of a course can be evaluated through the analysis of statistics relating to recruitment, retention and achievement. But statistics, though popular with those college managers who like to see graphs and charts in end of year reports, often mask more complex issues, and need to be accompanied by more detailed information.

Employer feedback

Again, from the point of view of a product model, we have to be aware of the feedback that is received from employers, who will expect certain standards of work or practice from those employees who have just achieved their qualifications. If there is a significant gap between the level of expertise or proficiency expected from the holder of an award, and from the company that has just given them a job, then in some way the curriculum will need revisiting. It may be the case that the qualification is simply inadequate. Or perhaps it is not sufficiently up to date.

Distance travelled

Many courses in the lifelong learning sector are not directly linked to employability, in the sense that students will complete the course and then step into a job. A group of students taking an NVQ level 2 in Beauty Therapy will not all go on to study at level 3, and only a small number of them may eventually work in the industry. But some of these students may, having discovered that being in education is a worthwhile activity, go on to further study within other curricula areas. A process view of curriculum, therefore, might seek to explore the extent to which students stay in education. Here, the focus is on the broader development of the students, above and beyond their certificates, and the curriculum is as much about showing what education and training can do for a person, as it is about content matter, skills and knowledge. When discussing individual student progress in this way, the phrase 'distance travelled' is often used. This term puts an explicit focus on the individual, personal progress of the student, notwithstanding their actual progress in terms of the qualification in question.

Moderation and verification

The internal moderation and external verification of assessment allows for a thorough evaluation of learning and teaching processes. Internal moderation tends to be peer-led and peer-supported. It can be quite an informal process, although the results of moderation are recorded formally. External verification by definition involves external scrutiny from a verifier who is appointed by the awarding body of the course in question. In addition to sampling assessed work, verifiers often ask to talk to students as well.

Students

We also need to be sensitive to the opinions of the students themselves. The ubiquitous end of term questionnaires serve a purpose, but there are other ways of finding out what students think of the courses that they are on. Staff–student panels are a common feature of curriculum provision in the lifelong learning sector. These provide a forum for a more detailed and sustained evaluation than is possible with a questionnaire. Care should be taken, however, to prevent a small minority of students from taking over such meetings in order to deliver what are essentially polemic statements, at the expense of meaningful evaluation and feedback. Data relating to the retention and attendance of students may also be revealing. A student who demonstrates a persistent pattern of absence may be having individual difficulties either with the course, or in their life more generally (or perhaps both). But a pattern of significant absenteeism on a particular course, from students who generally have good attendance records, may indicate a specific issue with that course.

Audit and inspection

At an institutional and governmental level, there is always a focus on achievement rates. But there is also a focus on value for money as well: after all, the taxpayer contributes significantly to the running costs of the lifelong learning sector. Audit and inspection can identify areas of financial mismanagement or waste. The mention of audit brings Ofsted to mind. We shall discuss Ofsted in a little more detail below, but it is worth remembering that Ofsted inspect not only teaching provision, but management provision as well. Stakeholders need to be confident that teaching is of a good quality. But they also need to know that the management structures that are in place within an institution are working correctly and efficiently in order to allow good teaching to happen.

Tutors

A commitment to a process or even a praxis model of curriculum demands that tutors evaluate their curricula, and their role within it, from a more personal and more theoretical perspective. End of term statistics and bar charts are one thing, but it could be argued that even complex sets of statistics cannot adequately capture the richness of the teaching and learning environment. The same goes for Ofsted: how realistic a picture can a short visit of a few days actually paint? Tutors can and should take some responsibility for evaluation, and this can be done through a commitment to reflective practice or even action research: these will be discussed below.

How should we evaluate?

There are several different ways by which a curriculum can be evaluated. Many of the methods that are commonly used in the lifelong learning sector will be quite familiar, even to relatively new teachers and trainers. They include:

- questionnaires;
- inspections;
- observations of teaching;
- staff–student committees;
- self-assessment reports;
- document audits.

So how are such methods applied in practice? If statistical evaluation is being carried out, then methods that generate statistics will of course be employed. A commonly used method is a questionnaire where questions are answered using a numerical scale, with 1 meaning 'strongly agree' and 5 meaning 'strongly disagree' (known as a 'Likert Scale'). Responses from all of the students completing the questionnaire can then be compiled and collated. An alternative approach would be to use existing sets of statistics. The use of computer-based systems for recording attendance, enrolment and achievement, for example, allows for such statistics to be quickly retrieved and analysed.

The evaluation of resources and facilities can also take place in a number of ways. Students can comment on resources in their questionnaires, or during staff–student meetings. Inspectors comment on available facilities. Awarding bodies may stipulate the levels of resources – staffing levels and staff qualifications, workshop facilities, rooms, library stocks – that they deem necessary for a course to run properly. External verifiers or examiners may ask for the perusal of such facilities to be included during a formal visit. It is also important to remember that resources and facilities that are not directly related to the course, such as catering facilities or recreational spaces, are also of importance. Similarly, Ofsted inspections always follow a particular set of processes, laid out in a document called *The Common Inspection Framework for inspecting education and training* (this can be downloaded in pdf format from the internet: a link to the document appears at the end of this chapter). The Common Inspection Framework is based around a series of key questions.

- How effective and efficient are the provision and related services in meeting the full range of learners' needs, and why?
- What steps need to be taken to improve the provision further?
- How well do learners achieve?
- How effective are teaching, training and learning?
- How well do programmes and activities meet the needs and interests of learners?
- How well are learners guided and supported?
- How effective are leadership and management in raising achievement and supporting all learners?

While lesson observations are perhaps the best known of the evaluation methods used by Ofsted, it is important to remember that an Ofsted inspection also involves the scrutiny of a considerable body of documentation, drawn from the institutions existing working practices.

Observations of teaching and self-assessment reports contribute to the Ofsted process: assessing the accuracy and validity of internal quality assurance processes is within Ofsted's remit. As such, it is hardly surprising that they are a very important part of any institutions internal evaluation systems. Writing a self-assessment report is generally a job for course leaders and managers, although other tutors may be asked to contribute. Observations of teaching sessions are more ubiquitous. Often, a college will have an established team of internal observers, who will observe lessons using the same criteria as Ofsted.

Where and when does evaluation happen?

Depending on how you define it, evaluation takes place both within and across institutions. It is an activity that occurs within a department or a faculty, a college or any other institution, or across a particular sector that might be defined regionally or institutionally. Some evaluations are deliberately local in outlook, and others have a national remit. Evaluation can be a formal process, wrapped up in systems and procedures, or it can be an informal process. Evaluation can occur at any time during the educational process.

Formal evaluation processes tend to happen at particular times in the year. Some examples are listed below.

- Self-assessment reports are usually written at the very start of the academic year, reporting on the year that has just finished.

- Observations of teaching and learning normally follow a schedule that has been agreed between college management and teaching staff.
- Student questionnaires are usually handed out at the end of term, and staff–student committees usually meet two or three times a year.
- External verifiers visit institutions at least once a year: these visits are often preceded by the writing of a report, or perhaps an audit of student portfolios.

These examples demonstrate the fact that evaluation can take place both during and after a course or programme of study. Consequently, the terms 'formative' and 'summative' can be applied to evaluation in the same way that they are applied to the assessment of student learning.

Stakeholders in the evaluation process

It is not just tutors, students and college managers who have an interest in how well educational provision is doing its job. If, as stated earlier, the curriculum is an area of legitimate interest for a wide range of people, including governments, employers, parents and guardians, then it follows that these groups of people will also be engaged at some level with the evaluation process. So, who are the different stakeholders in curriculum evaluation, and how are they specifically involved?

Teachers and trainers

It surely goes without saying that teachers in the learning and skills sector have a commitment to course and curriculum evaluation. Some aspects of the process can seem burdensome (such as the seemingly endless paperwork!) and other aspects can seem threatening (such as inspections). Nonetheless, an appreciation of why evaluation is important must be seen as an essential professional attribute.

College management

Managers – and principals – represent the point of connection between an institution and the outside world of employers, funding bodies and government agencies. It is therefore their responsibility to not only liaise with relevant external parties, but also establish and maintain appropriate internal evaluation and quality assurance procedures.

Students

Students are frequently and consistently encouraged to be part of the evaluation process, although the extent to which their involvement is meaningful can be a matter of debate (this issue is discussed in more detail below). The use that students make of the information that derives from evaluation is similarly debatable, and is perhaps linked to broader issues such as engagement and motivation (which are beyond the scope of this book).

Parents and guardians

The ways in which parents or guardians make use of evaluation information are also quite variable, and will depend not least on both simple facts such as the age of the student as well as more complex issues to do with family dynamics. Some students within the 14–19 age group, for example, will be accompanied by their parents to a college open evening. Other families will not attend at all. And I have lost count of the number of times a tutor has told me that the parents that they really want to see are the ones who never attend such public functions. Others are more involved: the investment in time, the contributions towards course fees and other financial aid, and broader support at home all lead to many parents continuing to take an active interest.

Examining and awarding bodies

Awarding bodies need to know that their curricula are being delivered properly, so that the integrity of the qualifications that they award can be assured. This integrity is important both for the users of the qualifications – students, employers, admissions tutors – and for those trade, industry or professional bodies and organisations that endorse specific qualifications.

Trade and industry representatives

As mentioned above, trade bodies and the like have a legitimate concern for the quality of qualifications that they endorse. But employers, in the wider sense, have a broader interest in the strength of the qualifications that they look or ask for in their employees. They need to be confident that an employee's qualifications accurately reflect their abilities and knowledge.

Funding agencies

Each year, several billions of pounds are spent by the Learning and Skills Council (LSC), which has been responsible for the funding and planning of learning in further education colleges, sixth form colleges, adult and community education centres and workplace education and training (for example through Train to Gain) since it began operating in 2001. Funding allocations and targets for achievement are given annually to the LSC by the government. In turn, providers are set targets by the LSC. These targets may relate to recruitment to specific courses, or to ensuring high attendance rates and low dropout rates.

Government bodies

And finally, it is worth remembering that the Department for Innovation, Universities and Skills ultimately sets the agenda that everyone in the lifelong learning sector works towards. Through the work of agencies such as the Quality Improvement Agency (QIA), the Institute for Learning (IFL), and the Learning and Skills Network (LSN), the government's agenda for the lifelong learning sector can be put into practice.

PRACTICAL TASK PRACTICAL TASK PRACTICAL TASK PRACTICAL TASK PRACTICAL TASK

Identifying and examining evaluation

By now, you should have a clear picture forming of those evaluation systems that impact on your professional practice. If you are already in employment in the sector, and are working towards QTLS by studying part-time, you may well have considerable experience of evaluation, even if your career in the sector has only recently begun. It is not unusual for relatively new tutors to be given responsibility for taking part in internal verification, or for writing self-assessment reports. If you are studying full-time you will probably not have had this experience, but your time spent on placement will provide plenty of opportunities for seeing evaluation systems at work.

So, look at all of the ways in which evaluation happens. Think about them critically, and consider how you might answer the following questions.

- What sorts of burdens do evaluation systems place on tutors, in terms of time spent on them and the stresses that they might cause?

- What happens to all the results of these evaluations? Are they actually acted on? Do they make a difference?

- To what extent are tutors told which evaluation systems to follow, and what kinds of evaluation do tutors choose to carry out themselves?

Unpacking evaluation

When talking with my teacher-training students about evaluation, Ofsted inspections invariably feature in our conversations. After the obligatory mix of complaint and suspicion, these conversations tend to settle down fairly quickly, provoking a more measured series of responses. The principles that underpin Ofsted inspections are in fact pretty widely accepted on such occasions: as one tutor said to me, *If you are doing your job well and properly, then what's the problem? I don't care who observes me, or when they do it*. Another tutor once said, *I like Ofsted because we always get a fresh coat of paint and some new pot plants*. This last comment might have been a joke (I was never too sure), but it summed up a more serious point. Just how realistic is an Ofsted inspection? How can Ofsted really be sure that what they see provides an authentic reflection of the institution that is being inspected? Or, to put it another way: how can we be sure of the validity and reliability of inspection, or of other evaluation processes?

Validity and reliability are two words that are used when discussing both assessment and research methods, as well as evaluation. Their meanings tend to remain fairly constant across these contexts. Here, validity refers to the extent to which the evaluation tool is actually evaluating the thing we want to evaluate. Reliability refers to the extent to which the same evaluation tool would obtain comparable and consistent results if it was used at a different time or in a different place. But there are other things to consider as well as the actual quality of the evaluation tool. Some evaluation methods are seen as helpful and supportive, and others are seen as intrusive and threatening. In sum, there are all sorts of ways in which evaluation processes can be critiqued, and we shall discuss some of these now.

Student evaluations

CLOSE FOCUS CLOSE FOCUS **CLOSE** FOCUS CLOSE FOCUS **CLOSE** FOCUS

A critique of student evaluation

Denis Hayes has written about student evaluations both from an FE perspective and an HE perspective. In an article he wrote three years ago for the *Times Educational Supplement*, he neatly summed up his argument thus:

> Student evaluations are entirely worthless. This is not an empirical point based on any research that looks at what they say. Such a project would be pointless. I'm making the logical point that to be able to evaluate a course, or even a lesson, students would need knowledge and skills at least equal, if not superior, to their lecturers. Not only do they not have the ability to evaluate, they cannot have it. It is just a false and flattering pretence to say that they have anything to say, or to ask them questions

of the easily quantifiable kind with which we are all familiar: 'The academic support on this course was very good, quite good, neither good nor bad, fairly poor, very poor, don't know.'

Students should all tick 'don't know' every time. That is the right answer.

Is this a legitimate criticism? Is it the case that students are simply neither knowledgeable nor qualified enough to make a meaningful judgement about their teachers or trainers? Do you think that you know enough about how teacher-training programmes work to give a valid evaluation of the course that you are currently following?

It could be argued that the basis for engaging students in the evaluation process is that they are perceived as being customers of a product – an educational course or programme – and that the vendor – the institution attended by the student – wants to be sure that the customer is happy. And so students are given end of term questionnaires, start of term questionnaires and even sometimes mid-term questionnaires. Student representatives meet college governors. Staff–student liaison committees meet two or three times each year. But how useful is it to hear the student voice? Does it make a real difference?

Evaluation: who really benefits?

One of the more difficult aspects of the evaluation of teaching and learning is the issue of observations. These are ubiquitous within further education colleges and are an increasingly common feature of adult and community education practice as well. Tutors are almost always warned in advance that they will be observed and observation teams are normally made up of appropriately qualified members of staff. However, this is not always the case. The presence of poor professional experience or qualifications among team members can destabilise observation procedures and damage the credibility of the process. Observations are intended to generate meaningful and constructive feedback, so that the tutor can develop or improve their practice, as appropriate. But they are also graded, normally using a grading system that is copied from Ofsted. Some tutors do not worry about this: others find the whole notion of being graded worrying, even threatening, and as such the developmental aspect of the process is weakened.

Evaluation, managerialism and performativity

There is a significant body of research that has explored the post-compulsory sector from the linked perspectives of managerialism and performativity. Here, managerialism is defined as an ethos of management within an organisation where such management helps the organisation in question to be as productive as it can possibly be, in as efficient a way as possible, overriding any alternative perspectives based on a professional ethos (Tummons, 2007). Performativity is defined as a culture of workplace organisation where management impose systems based around targets, accountability, and a *blame culture* (Avis, 2005).

If we accept these arguments, then the role of evaluation within an organisation becomes less about a meaningful exploration of courses and curricula, and more about processes of surveillance and interference in the working lives of tutors. Evaluation procedures exist because tutors cannot be trusted to make sound and reliable value judgements. Rather, these judgements need to be generated and managed using systems that have been imposed on tutors, rather than created by them.

Summarising evaluation

Whether or not we accept arguments relating to managerialism and performativity, or the usefulness of inspections and observations, it is evident that the bureaucracy that surrounds evaluation tends to obscure the reasons why it is there in the first place. There is so much focus on the paperwork and procedures that the real act of evaluation gets lost sight of. So what are the alternatives?

Evaluation and the tutor: reflective practice and action research

There are two aspects of a tutor's or teacher's professional practice that can be seen as contributing to evaluation, although this would not necessarily be their main focus: reflective practice, and action research. These are activities that will be familiar to some of us from other contexts. Reflective practice, for example, is a core theme of many teacher-training curricula within the learning and skills sector. Action research, though less well known within teacher-training curricula, is found in a variety of professional and higher education courses.

Reflective practice

Reflective practice is a state of mind, a permanent kind of behaviour. It is a practice that encourages a careful and honest appraisal of any and all of the situations and phenomena that a teacher or trainer might encounter in their professional lives. In this sense, being a reflective practitioner involves a constant, critical appraisal of teaching and learning, as well as of the work of a teacher or trainer more generally. Reflective practice is a way of exploring and picking apart all those aspects of teaching that get taken for granted. In sum, it is a key component of the teacher's professional make-up.

It follows, therefore, that part of the remit of reflective practice would be the evaluation of particular kinds of learning and teaching issues. Indeed, it seems unavoidable. But this kind of reflection can and should move beyond the immediate issues that arise in a workshop or classroom. A technical level of reflection, with a focus on nuts and bolts issues, will only get us so far. A more critical level of reflection provides the theoretical frameworks needed to consider broader issues relating to our teaching, and our curricula.

Theory focus

Stephen Brookfield

According to Brookfield (1985) there are four critical lenses for reflecting on practice:

1. the point of view of the practitioner: our own perspective;
2. the point of view of our learners;
3. the point of view of our colleagues;
4. the point of view of established theory.

Brookfield is interested in what he terms assumptions; those things which we do, and those things that influence the things that we do, that we never really think about or ask questions about. A willingness to unpack such assumptions, which have powerful advocates in many different contexts in the learning and skills sector (and in the wider education sector as a whole, in fact) is what characterises critical reflection. In this critical form, reflective practice focuses on broader, more

---

profound issues as well: those issues that have an impact on learning and teaching that are to be found outside the immediate confines of a college or adult education centre. Brookfield has a concern for the political and the social, those broader forces that impact on our curricula.

Brookfield's *critical lenses* is not the only model of reflective practice that can be used to help reflections move from the technical to the critical. But it is a good way to illustrate the point. Suggested reading on reflective practice more generally can be found at the end of this chapter.

Action research

We have already talked about action research in Chapters 1 and 2 of this book, and so here we shall only briefly revise the key themes of action research before explaining why it belongs in a discussion about evaluation. Action research can be defined as a small-scale enquiry undertaken by practitioners – in our context, teachers and trainers – that is carried out with the aim of changing or improving something. For the purposes of our discussion, the 'something' would be a curriculum, or a curriculum component. The potential overlap between action research and evaluation is quite unambiguous. An action research project would almost always involve an element of evaluation – of the original curriculum, of the changes that you wish to make, of the impact of those changes on your students and your teaching – that offers a rich insight into your professional practice more generally.

However, action research takes time and effort. Some teacher–training courses offer students the option to carry out a piece of small-scale research, but it is more common in other programmes: foundation degrees or part-time BA programmes, for example. It can be very difficult for a busy full-time college tutor to find the time to carry out such work, or for a part-time adult education tutor to justify the level of work required when teaching is only a small part of what they do. It is certainly slower than asking students to fill in questionnaires, or any of the other procedures preferred by college managers who are keen to make sure that their tutors are working as efficiently as possible. Sadly, college managers do not always seem to appreciate the value of work such as this. But if, after finishing teacher-training, you go on to further study, then carrying out an action research project would prove to be a worthwhile and valuable experience.

A SUMMARY OF **KEY POINTS**

In this chapter we have looked at the following key themes:

> **definitions of evaluation;**

> **methods and scope of carrying out evaluation;**

> **stakeholders in the evaluation process;**

> **issues of debate around the practice of evaluation;**

> **reflective practice and action research as methods for evaluation.**

The practice of evaluation is all-pervasive in the lifelong learning sector, whether we are discussing accredited evening classes for adults or the provision of higher education courses in a further education context. There are different regimes and systems that perform evaluation, and different ways of thinking about how evaluation impacts on teaching staff.

But when all is said and done, it is unavoidable; and so, as teachers and trainers, we need to work with those evaluation systems that make sense at a professional level, and continue to debate those which might be seen as needlessly burdensome.

Branching options
Reflection

Consider the ways in which evaluation is carried out within the organisation that you work in and by the curricular bodies and agencies that you deal with. To what extent do you think these evaluation methods are chosen because they provide meaningful data that generates a real insight into how well a curriculum is doing?

Analysis

The ways in which differing evaluation methods and regimes can be implemented and justified vary according to who is doing the implementation and justification. To what extent do you feel that you are an active participant in the evaluation processes that you find yourself working in?

Research

Reflective practice and action research are important areas of professional and scholarly activity, and are worth following up in their own right. In terms of evaluation more generally, further research into management cultures in the lifelong learning sector would allow for a more sustained critique of evaluation, and suggestions for reading appear below.

REFERENCES AND FURTHER READING REFERENCES AND FURTHER READING

Avis, J. (2005) Beyond performativity: reflections on activist professionalism and the labour process in further education. *Journal of Education Policy,* 20(2): 209–222.

Brookfield, S. (1985) *Becoming a Critically Reflective Teacher.* San Francisco: Jossey-Bass.

Hayes, D. and Wynyard, R. (2006) (eds) *The McDonaldization of Higher Education.* Charlotte, North Carolina: IAP.

Moon, J. (1999) *Reflection in Learning and Professional Development.* Abingdon: RoutledgeFalmer.

Tummons, J. (2007) *Becoming a Professional Tutor in the Lifelong Learning Sector.* Exeter: Learning Matters.

Websites

The Ofsted common inspection framework can be found at:
www.ofsted.gov.uk/content/download/4576/37815/file/Common%20Inspection%20Framework %20for%20inspecting%20education%20and%20training%20(PDF%20format).pdf

Denis Hayes's article can be found at:
www.tes.co.uk/article.aspx?storycode=2142732

And the websites for those government agencies mentioned in this chapter are:
www.lsc.gov.uk/
www.dius.gov.uk/

6
Curriculum, learning and knowledge

By the end of this chapter you should:

- have a developing understanding of different theoretical frameworks related to knowledge;
- be able to start applying these knowledge models to curriculum theory.

Professional Standards

This chapter relates to the following Professional Standards:

Professional Values:

DS 1 Planning to promote equality, support diversity and to meet the aims and learning needs of learners.

DS 2 Learner participation in the planning of learning.

Professional Knowledge and Understanding:

DK 2.1 The importance of including learners in the planning process.

Professional Practice:

DP 1.1 Plan coherent and inclusive learning programmes that meet learners' needs and curriculum requirements, promote equality and engage with diversity effectively.

This chapter will allow you to work towards the following elements of the *LLUK Minimum Core*:

Language and Literacy – Personal Language Skills
Reading:

- Find, and select from, a range of reference material and sources of information, including the internet.
- Use and reflect on a range of reading strategies to interpret texts and to locate information or meaning.
- Identify and record the key information or messages contained within reading material using note-taking techniques.

Introduction

Up to this point, we have looked at some definitions of curriculum and some key concepts to help us explore it. We have thought about some of the different social and political factors that have an impact on curriculum. These are broadly theoretical issues, although practical examples and themes have been discussed as well. At a more overtly practical level, we have considered how examples of real-life curricula are actually planned and delivered in a workshop and classroom context, and the different ways by which curricula are evaluated. In this chapter, we shall return to some more theoretical issues. These are illustrated through real-life case studies, but it is also important to remember that some of the issues raised in this chapter impact on other areas of the QTLS curriculum, particularly relating to theories of learning.

Learning theory is a broad area of study and research, and is treated differently by different writers. Different theories and approaches are hotly disputed. As such, it is an impossible task to summarise adequately the whole of such a diverse body of scholarship. Here, a more selective approach will be taken. Some areas of research will not be considered in this chapter. Among the absentees is andragogy, variously defined as the art and science of teaching adults (Knowles, 1970). While some books spend much time on this subject, I am happy to refer to Peter Jarvis who has questioned *why Knowles' work, which is so obviously wrong when applied to children and adults, has retained so much currency* (1995, p198). Detailed analyses of many of the 'isms' (behaviourism, cognitivism, humanism) that are a common feature of other teacher-training textbooks are also absent in this book, because they are indeed so common. I am assuming that the majority of readers will have explored learning theories at an earlier stage in their studies towards QTLS. Appropriate references are included at the end of this chapter which will allow the interested reader to explore any particular theoretical approach in more depth. Instead, I shall consider learning theories from a perspective that allows us to think about knowledge. That is to say, the major focus of this chapter is knowledge and knowing, and how these are reflected in curricula, and learning theories are referred to only as they relate to these.

Why do we need to spend time thinking about knowledge and knowing? Quite simply, because if a curriculum is about anything at all (allowing for the different and sometimes conflicting definitions and issues that we have looked at so far), it is about one key thing:

> people who know something (and they might be called teachers or trainers, but need not be) showing or helping some other people (who might be called students or learners, but need not be) to learn how to do that something as well as they can themselves. The curriculum is the framework, setting or context that embodies and enfolds the *something*.

When I write *know something*, I mean this in the broadest sense, relating to knowing how to do things or knowing about particular subjects or topics. It could be *knowing* how to disassemble a Sturmey Archer 3-speed hub gear, or *knowing* how to translate correctly into English a piece of poetry that has been written in Spanish. It could be *knowing* how to put together a PowerPoint presentation, or how to repair the lead flashing at the bottom of a chimney stack. Whether we talk about practical and theory, or knowledge and understanding and ability, it all comes down to knowing how to do particular things in certain ways and at appropriate times. So we need to spend time thinking about what knowledge is, what we think it means when we say that *we know something*, and how this informs our point of view when it comes to delivering or interpreting a curriculum. But to get to this question, we need to start by thinking about what learning is.

Thinking about learning
What is learning?

What does it mean when we say that we have learned something new or learned how to do something? What are the processes involved and how can we recognise that learning is happening? Are other people involved in helping us do some learning, or does it happen on an entirely personal level? Learning chemistry at school somehow seems to be a completely different thing to learning how to drive or learning how to use a computer but they are all kinds of 'learning' that I have done. In fact even these three examples provide more questions than answers. I can't remember any of my O level chemistry apart from a few formulae and equations that aren't really much use on their own. And after I had passed my driving test, my driving instructor said to me something along the lines of *Well, now that you have passed your test, you'll really* learn *how to drive*, a statement that implied that the really important or useful learning about driving was going to happen with me on my own in the car. And the last time I attended a formal computer course was when I was ten years old, and the computers were very different then. The only thing I remember was that I wrote a computer programme that calculated Fibonacci numbers (and, perhaps inevitably, I can't remember what they actually are). So how did I learn how to download music from the internet (legally, of course) and install software on my laptop?

REFLECTIVE TASK
REFLECTIVE TASK

What is learning?
You will have your own ideas and preconceptions about learning. This might be in terms of what it is, how and where it happens, what might help or impede it and who needs to be involved. There may be other factors as well. These ideas may have been formed from your own experiences as a student (including your experiences as a student who is working towards QTLS), perhaps as a teacher or trainer in employment or on a placement, or perhaps outside formal educational settings, such as learning about a hobby or other interest. Spend a moment thinking about how you define learning, and how you define the 'stuff' that we all learn.

What is learning, then? It seems to involve both theoretical things (ideas, facts, concepts), practical things (physical actions and gestures), and things that are to do with attitude as well (being a safe and vigilant driver). Learning can happen in formal contexts, where a teacher, instructor or facilitator is present, although the exact relationship between teaching and learning is far from straightforward. In addition, it would seem that the things that we have been learning have a 'best before date': in other words, we can learn things that we later forget. How quickly this forgetting happens would seem to depend on at least two key factors: how often we practise the thing we have just learned, and how much effort we actually put into learning it in the first place. So, in this sense, learning is something we need to keep working at. But there is also the sense that we can get better at learning the more we do it, and that if we do forget things, we might have the option of 'getting it back' later. And although much learning takes place in formal educational institutions, a lot of other learning does not.

In his book *How We Learn*, Knud Illeris provides us with a definition that is both broad and useful, and is the definition that I shall work with here. For Illeris, learning is:

> ... *any process that in living organisms leads to permanent capacity change and which is not solely due to biological maturation or aging.*

> (Illeris, 2007, p3)

Knowledge: the stuff that we learn

So, what are we learning? What's the actual 'stuff' that we are learning when we sit in a class and do some group work, or listen to a tutor, or read something on a web page or in a book? And where does this stuff actually end up? In our heads? Somewhere else? These kinds of questions allow us to start making links between different theoretical approaches to learning, and different approaches to knowledge.

Where is the 'stuff' that we learn?

There are essentially two approaches to learning, and all of the 'isms' and 'ologies' can be seen as belonging – on a sliding scale – to one or the other.

1. At one end of the scale are approaches to learning that are individual. That is to say, learning is understood as an individual, cognitive process, and we learn by receiving. Such approaches (*behaviourism* and *neo-behaviourism*, for example) view the learner as a passive recipient, being 'filled up' with skills or knowledge by the teaching process.
2. At the other end of the scale are theories of learning as being socially situated. That is to say, learning is understood as something that we all do all of the time, as we go about our lives. Such approaches (*communities of practice* and *activity theory*, for example) view the learner as being actively involved in the learning process, making meaning for themselves rather than being filled up with someone else's under-standings.
3. However, in the middle are some theories of learning that are based on the individual, but acknowledge the role of the social world in helping learning to occur. Such approaches (*cognitivism* and *social constructivism*, for example) view learning as an individual cognitive process, although this process is influenced and informed by social interaction.

And depending which approach to learning you take, then the stuff that we learn – we'll call this knowledge – is treated differently.

1. Individual approaches (behaviourism and cognitivism) to learning focus knowledge on the individual. That is to say, in some way the things that we know are in our heads and we pull them out when we need to do so.
2. Socially situated approaches to learning place knowledge in society. That is to say, in some way the things that we know are shared in society and the world at large, and we can plug into them, draw from them, contribute to them and share them as and when we need to.

Is all knowledge the same?

There are as many different ways of thinking about knowledge as there are of thinking about learning. Learning theories dictate where we think knowledge actually 'is'. Other theories of knowledge and competence provide us with ways of thinking about what we might refer to as different sorts of knowledge. This is a big topic, and so here I shall provide a brief outline of those more relevant approaches that help generate a working model of knowledge use for the teacher or trainer.

Technical, practical and professional knowledge

In his book *Developing Professional Knowledge and Competence*, Michael Eraut discusses a number of ways in which different kinds of knowledge have been theorised. For example, there is a distinction to be drawn between *technical knowledge* and *practical knowledge* (a distinction that goes back to Aristotle, in fact). Technical knowledge is the kind of knowledge that you can actually write down – in a curriculum document, series of occupational standards, or textbook, for example. Practical knowledge is learned through experience, when actually doing the job, and can only really be seen at work in practice. And then there is *professional knowledge*, which is the specific knowledge required by professionals to carry out their work to the standards expected by both other members of the profession, and users of the services provided by the profession. In many ways, therefore, professional knowledge can be seen as resting on both technical and practical knowledge. Or, to put it another way, professional knowledge is based on both qualifications and experience.

Tacit knowledge and knowing-in-action

Michael Polanyi, in his book *The Tacit Dimension*, suggests that people can be in possession of particular kinds of knowledge that are quite real, but incapable of being written down or even spoken about. Such knowledge is there, but hidden. He uses the term *tacit knowledge* to describe this (tacit is defined in the *Oxford English Dictionary* as *understood or implied without being stated*). Polanyi's concept of tacit knowledge serves as a foundation stone for Donald Schön's concept of *knowing-in-action*, the kinds of knowledge that are revealed as we go about actions in a skilful manner, and which are developed through both academic study and reflective practice.

Workplace knowledge

John Stevenson has written several articles relating to *workplace knowledge*. He suggests that the changing nature of the workplace, in the broadest meaning of the term, has resulted in particular kinds of workplace knowledge. The growth of flexible working, the casualisation of the workforce, the loss of the *job for life* and the need to up-skill and re-skill are all aspects of contemporary working practices that have a subsequent impact on the knowledge that people need in the workplace. Workplace knowledge is not just about being expert in one industrial sector or trade specialism: it is about being able to learn new things at work and adapt to new working practices. Consequently, we can talk about workplace knowledge being embedded within a workplace curriculum which workers, as learners, may participate in both formally (through formal training, for example) and informally (through 'learning on the job').

Teacher knowledge

Lee Shulman has written extensively about what he terms teacher knowledge. This is obviously a variety of knowledge that is immediately of interest to anyone working towards QTLS while reading this book. Shulman makes the important distinction between *content knowledge* and *pedagogical content knowledge*. Content knowledge is the stuff that teachers already know about their subject or area of competence or expertise: this might be accountancy, carpentry or horticulture. Pedagogical context knowledge is a variation of this, and refers to the ways in which teachers have to convert or transfer their content knowledge into a form that can then be taught to their students. A third kind of teacher knowledge is *curricular knowledge*. This refers to the broader knowledge about the curriculum as a whole that, according to Shulman, teachers need to know about. This broader curricular knowledge allows teachers to make meaningful links between the course or programme that they work with, and the wider curriculum that their students are exposed to as a consequence of their participation in education and training.

Knowledge: the stuff that we know and teach

In our lives as teachers and trainers, we draw on different kinds of knowledge as we go about our work within the curricula that we teach. In order to deliver a curriculum, we need different kinds of knowledge. We need to know the subject matter. But we also need to know about that subject matter in a way that can best be delivered to a group of students. And we need to know about pedagogy, so that we have the appropriate understanding of learning and teaching processes to allow us to work successfully with our students. Or, to put it another way, we need to be qualified (with whatever qualifications are appropriate) both in our subjects, and as teachers as well. So how might we see or understand these different types of knowledge work in practice?

CASE STUDY
Tutors at work

Wendy and Jane both work as lecturers in beauty therapy at a further education college. Wendy works at the college's main buildings, in a working salon that has been recently refurbished. Her students come from across the city, and are working towards industry-recognised qualifications at levels 2 and 3. They tend to be school-leavers, although a small number of adults who are planning to either re-enter the workplace or change careers also attend. Jane works off-site in a small community education building in the middle of a large housing estate. Here, resources and facilities are quite limited. Her students are working towards a level 2 qualification. They come from the local community. For the most part, they are adult returners to learning, often overcoming considerable social and personal barriers in order to attend.

In the two passages that follow, particular examples of critical moments that occurred during a teaching session have been highlighted. Wendy and Jane are both teaching theory sessions – anatomy and physiology ('a and p'). As you read through these passages, consider how they draw on different kinds of knowledge as they work with their students.

Wendy

Level 2 today. The a and p is sometimes hard work for the girls when they are at this stage, but I was quite pleased with today's session. I'd taken on board my course leader's suggestion about their phones, and made sure that they had all handed them in at the start – less fuss than I thought there would be, and loads less interruptions. So we did group work and they all had a different skin condition to research using the internet, and then they drew up posters which they could show to everyone else. Took a bit longer than I thought though. But they all found out some useful things which they could tell the rest of us, and then I put my slides up. The photos went down well, although a couple of the girls were a bit queasy. Some of the girls had stories from work about meeting clients with these kinds of conditions and I gave some examples as well from both my salon and the training salon about possible treatments and times when I have had to make referrals to GPs. I think these helped to really make it stick.

Jane

The students were fairly quiet again today – I think they are finding the underpinning theory a bit of a shock to the system. When I got the Lorraine Nordmann books for them all the other week I think they went into shock because it's quite big. But it's such a good book! Anyway, they hadn't all done their worksheets from last time so we had to go through them and it got a bit better as we went on. Some of them had some writing to do, and some had diagrams to label and finish off and then I went round the class asking questions to check understanding. When I told them what we'd be doing in the practical session I think that helped a bit because it refers back to the last session as well.

While we were all tidying away before lunch Sara came over to talk to me. She always makes me worry – she's one of the two students who I keep thinking will just not turn up one day and it's only a small group as it is. But she wasn't worrying or complaining at all – she was being really positive and saying thanks for last time when we'd had to have a big talk after the session. But the funny thing is that I can't really remember what we talked about even though it was nearly an hour. I must have said something right!

Discussion

So, what kinds of knowledge might Wendy and Jane be drawing on here? Wendy's professional knowledge as a practising beauty therapist rests on two distinct platforms: the technical knowledge gained from her extensive qualifications and continuing professional development, and the practical knowledge gained from several years' experience of running both her own salon and working in the training salon. Both of these bodies of knowledge complement each other. The practical knowledge acquired in the workplace (which we could refer to, therefore, as workplace knowledge) enhances the technical knowledge acquired during formal study which, no matter how thorough the curriculum, can (it could be argued) never quite prepare students for the reality of day-to-day working life.

Wendy's content knowledge – all of that expertise and understanding that relates to the beauty therapy industry – is transformed into a format that her students can understand. It becomes pedagogic content knowledge. Wendy does this by drawing on her knowledge and understanding of learning and teaching – the professional knowledge she has acquired through her teaching qualifications and experience. And finally she is able to contextualise the unit that her students are currently working on in terms of both the level 2 qualification, and the beauty therapy curriculum as a whole. She does this by drawing on her curricular knowledge, the thorough understanding and awareness that she has of the qualifications structure, the curriculum in general, and the way that it meets the requirements of the awarding body, the professional body and industry generally.

Jane is also drawing on these different kinds of knowledge. This is perhaps unsurprising. She shares Wendy's professional background, they have similar qualifications and broadly similar experiences both in the beauty therapy industry, and in education and training. But there is an additional aspect to Jane's reflections that touches on an aspect of knowledge that Wendy does not, at this time, hint at: her conversation with and support for her student, Sara. Sara shares some of the concerns and worries that are perhaps more common among adult returners to learning than among school-leavers going into further education. The kinds of issues faced by adult returners have been written about extensively elsewhere and will not be rehearsed in depth here, but can involve concerns over childcare, motivation, self-esteem and financial worries (Rogers, 2007). Irrespective of whether or not a tutor takes an overtly humanistic approach to their work, helping students cope with issues such as these is a common feature of the tutor's professional practice. Being approached by a student at the end of a session obviously does not give a tutor any time to consider or prepare a response, yet Jane has clearly managed to allay Sara's worries.

Teacher-training courses do try to prepare students for this pastoral aspect of the tutor's work. Indeed, there is a small but growing body of research to suggest that such *emotional labour* is becoming an increasingly significant part of being a tutor (Avis and Bathmaker, 2004). But it is understandably difficult for a teacher-training programme to anticipate all of the difficulties and dilemmas of everyday life that might have an impact on the students that we work with in the lifelong learning sector. The sheer diversity of students in terms of age (14–16-year-old groups; 16–19 groups; adults at various stages in their lives or careers), social background or prior educational experience, to name just three factors, means that it is very difficult for even the most well-designed QTLS programmes to cover all eventualities. Jane's sympathetic understanding of Sara's problems is certainly informed to some extent by the knowledge that she acquired during her teacher training: from the course itself, from the experiences of her fellow students and of her tutor (all in their turn informed by lots of different knowledge bases). But her own experiences – at work, in life, in the home – will surely also play a part. Jane is able to draw on all of these different kinds of knowledge. It is not at all clear exactly how she knows what to say, how to say it and when to do so, as she talks with Sara. But she certainly knows what is needed.

It seems right to describe this aspect of her understanding as being based on tacit knowledge. It would be difficult, if not impossible, for Jane – or for anyone in a similar situation – to unpack exactly what goes on during such exchanges. Jane's responses to Sara as they talk at the end of the session are fluid, fluent and deeply personal. They are also unique to this particular moment. As she listens to and reassures her student, Jane is drawing on a highly individual wealth of knowledge and experience, blended together seamlessly and perhaps even unconsciously, in a manner that is difficult to define, or, to put it another way, is tacit.

Theories of knowledge and theories of curriculum

So far so good. But we now need to return to the study of curriculum, and explore the links between different theories of knowledge and different theories of curriculum. More specifically, we need to think about how the different kinds of knowledge that we have explored here can be mapped onto the different understandings of curriculum that we have looked at in earlier chapters in this book. We can do this through a close-up focus on real-life case studies.

> ## CASE STUDY
> **BTEC national certificate in electrical/electronic engineering**
> In Chapter 4, we looked at this BTEC curriculum as our first case study when exploring the more practical aspects of curriculum organisation: resources, sequencing and people. Here, our focus is more theoretical, relating to the kinds of knowledge that the successful delivery of this curriculum might draw on.
>
> The BTEC National Diploma in Electrical and Electronic Engineering is a qualification that is designed to map onto the national occupational standards required by SEMTA (the Sector Skills Council for Science, Engineering and Manufacturing Technologies).

The award consists of a mixture of core and optional units, and the course is intended to be delivered in educational institutions such as FE colleges. This BTEC course is work-related, not work-based. This is an important distinction: it means that this BTEC does not claim to provide occupational competence, which can only be delivered in an authentic work context, not in an educational institution. Rather, it places itself as providing appropriate underpinning knowledge and a thorough grounding in workplace practice that the learners will be able to draw on when involved in future work-based learning such as when working towards an NVQ.

What kinds of knowledge might be involved in delivering this curriculum?

The *dual professionalism* of tutors has already been referred to in this chapter, and I have written about this elsewhere (Tummons, 2007). Here, it is sufficient to note that tutors tend to be qualified both in their subject specialism, and as tutors. In addition, many of the tutors who work within technical or vocational curricula such as electrical and electronic engineering tend to have considerable industrial experience as well. They may have worked for large companies, or owned their own businesses. Indeed, it is quite common for tutors to maintain links to business or industry while working in colleges. This might be through regular work, or simply through CPD. This combination of qualifications (technical knowledge) and experience (practical knowledge, accrued in the workplace) therefore allows tutors to develop a considerable body of professional knowledge, *as electrical and electronic engineers*. So how do we travel from professional knowledge to teacher knowledge?

Such a thorough grounding in the subject provides tutors with content knowledge. The tutors also possess professional knowledge as tutors, again built on both qualifications and experience. This aspect of teacher knowledge gives our tutors a particular understanding of the subject and so they are able to take what they know, as engineers, and explain and explore it with students in such a way that learning can be facilitated. The tutors know which order to explain things in, which examples to use and which practical tasks to set because they have the appropriate pedagogical content knowledge. And they know how the subject fits into the broader engineering curriculum, as well as how it fits into wider curricular demands such as key skills, because of their curricular knowledge – their understanding of how the qualification works in the context of the wider learning and skills sector.

Which models and concepts can help us explore this curriculum?

In terms of curriculum content – knowledge and understanding, aspects of occupational competence, theories and skills – several models can be applied: the planned curriculum; the official curriculum; the formal curriculum. Although there are some subtle differences between them, these concepts all essentially relate to the formal programme of study as it has been designed by the awarding body (in this case, Edexcel) so that it meets the requirements of the relevant industrial sector. The curriculum consists (in part) of a specified body of knowledge that has been shaped in such a way that it is appropriate for industry, meets the needs of the students in terms of planned learning and assessment activities, and is designed in such a way that it can be properly and correctly delivered by any suitably resourced college or training centre that has been approved to deliver the award.

Of more interest, perhaps, is the potential for slippage between the way that the curriculum is planned, and the way that the curriculum is received or experienced. A specified curriculum with a list of aims, outcomes and requirements is all well and good, but still needs to be actually put into practice by people – by tutors and students. In the real world, different tutors will invariably deliver aspects of the curriculum in slightly different ways. This might depend on the depth of their own experience, or on their own preferences and interests. Some tutors may be rich in technical knowledge and will consider its delivery as the sole aim of their teaching. Other tutors may wish to impress wider issues or values on their students. Curriculum delivery may vary according to the extent of the tutor's own content knowledge: it is not unknown for a hard-pushed line manager to ask a member of staff to take over a course that they are not exactly qualified to teach. It may vary according to the preferences or prejudices of the tutor, expressed through a hidden curriculum. In sum, how a curriculum is actually delivered will depend in great part on the actual tutor.

The particular dynamics of a student group will also make a difference. If a tutor's own knowledge can be used to 'stretch' aspects of the curriculum, then the responses of the students to that curriculum can also be seen as a factor. Studying the 'communications for technicians' unit, for example, can be seen as being both straightforward and immediately relevant. The need to use and interpret technical drawings has an obvious practical application. The 'business systems for technicians' unit, by contrast, may well provide tutors with lots of opportunities for embedding key skills (the unit includes a costing exercise that covers application of number) but may not quite be what students were expecting to learn when enrolling on an electrical engineering course. A tutor who ran their own business may well be able to offer insights into the ways that legislation impacts on the operations of an engineering company, but a debate on the wider economic environment, and how it affects an engineering company, may well lack relevance to some students (and may well be outside the professional knowledge base of some tutors). Due to factors like these, we can explore the gaps between any planned curriculum and the received or experienced curriculum.

CASE STUDY
NCFE level 2 NVQ in Advice, Guidance and Support

Once again, our focus here is on some of the theoretical issues relating to concepts of knowledge and curriculum as they might be applied to this NCFE award.

The NCFE level 2 NVQ in Advice, Guidance and Support is a work-based qualification (as opposed to a work-related qualification). The award has been designed by NCFE with appropriate reference to three other organisations: the Institute of Customer Service (ICS: the independent professional body for customer service); Skills for Care and Development (SfC&D: the Sector Skills Council for social care, children and young people's workforces); and ENTO (once known as The Employment National Training Organisation, but now known solely as ENTO), the standards setting body for advice and guidance. As this is a work-based NVQ, simulation is not allowed to be part of the assessment process. Rather, assessment must be based on authentic working practices. As such, the NCFE curriculum documents stress the requirements for assessors to be occupationally competent and qualified, as well as qualified to assess (through holding an A1 Assessor's Award).

What kinds of knowledge might be involved in delivering this curriculum?

In many ways, this NVQ demands similar kinds of knowledge to the BTEC award that we have already explored. Using the language of NVQs, we can say that meeting the under-pinning theory outcomes will draw on technical knowledge, and the ability outcomes will draw on practical knowledge. The assessor occupies a dual professional role, drawing on both occupational expertise relating to advice and guidance, as well as the specific expertise attached to the assessor role. This dual professionalism will be somewhat different to the role taken by the BTEC tutor, however. An assessor is not the same as a tutor: there are significant differences in the responsibilities that the role requires. As such it could be argued that the requirements for the use of pedagogical content knowledge are different in this instance because the assessor is not actually teaching. Content knowledge remains impor-tant because this forms the basis on which the assessor can make a professional judgement. And, finally, it can be argued that workplace knowledge plays a key role here. Advice and guidance providers, like any organisations, will have different ways of going about things, different systems and procedures and the like. An understanding of the variability or flex-ibility of such provision, of the different ways that things are done in different settings, can best be understood through reference to workplace knowledge.

Which models and concepts can help us explore this curriculum?

An NVQ that is based on authentic workplace practices, rather than college-based activities, raises several areas of discussion that make it quite different, from the perspective of curriculum studies, to a BTEC in Electrical and Electronic Engineering. To understand fully a work-based NVQ, we need to return to the concept of the workplace curriculum that was introduced in Chapter 4 (Billett, 2006).

Drawing on the workplace curriculum model, we can make a number of assumptions. We can assume that an employee who has been asked to work towards an NVQ either has already or will be given sufficient work experience for the core units and for selected optional units (we shall return to the optional units later) to be properly contextualised. That is to say, it would be impossible for a candidate to achieve the NVQ if they were not being allowed to take part in the appropriate workplace practices, routines and activities. This can be termed the intended workplace curriculum. Unfortunately, some companies and employers are less inclined or less able to support candidates sufficiently, and as such the candidate might not have access to those work routines that are needed to demonstrate competence. This can be defined as the enacted workplace curriculum.

And finally, the NVQ allows us to consider an application of negotiated curriculum. While acknowledging that for some writers in this subject, a genuinely negotiated curriculum would be entirely the responsibility of the learner, the provision of a qualification based on core and optional units does nonetheless allow the candidate to express some prefer-ences of areas for accreditation, assuming that they can negotiate appropriate work experience.

A SUMMARY OF **KEY POINTS**

In this chapter we have looked at the following key themes:

> **theories of learning and theories of knowledge;**

> **the links between theories of knowledge and curriculum theory;**

> **the ways in which these theories can be used to analyse real-world educational settings.**

The two case studies that have been used in this chapter are by no means exhaustive. It would take many, many examples from the different parts of the lifelong learning sector to explore fully the concepts of knowledge, and the related concepts of curriculum, that have been discussed here. The intention here was to provide a gateway for analysis that can hopefully be applied by practitioners from across these different contexts.

Branching options

Reflection

Think about how these models of knowledge apply to you. Consider the different ways in which your dual professional knowledge has been acquired or developed over time. To what extent does that knowledge change and adapt still?

Analysis

One way to unpack the relationships between different types or kinds of knowledge would be to trace the exact relationships between one aspect of your content knowledge and the corresponding body of pedagogical content knowledge. Consider how a body of knowledge – and this can be theoretical or practical – changes shape or form as you decide how and when different aspects of that body of knowledge should be taught.

Research

Theories of knowledge are worth pursuing should time and inclination allow, not least because much significant work (Eraut and Shulman in particular) has been done relating to teachers' knowledge. The recommended reading below is only a very partial list, but should allow for thorough coverage of the key debates.

REFERENCES AND FURTHER READING REFERENCES AND FURTHER READING

Avis, J. and Bathmaker, A-M. (2004) The politics of care: emotional labour and trainee further education lecturers. *Journal of Vocational Education and Training,* 56(1): 5–20.

Billett, S. (2006) Constituting the workplace curriculum. *Journal of Curriculum Studies,* 38(1): 31–48.

Eraut, M. (1994) *Developing Professional Knowledge and Competence*. Abingdon: RoutledgeFalmer.

Illeris, K. (2007) *How We Learn. Learning and non-learning in school and beyond.* London: Routledge.

Jarvis, P. (1995) *Adult and Continuing Education: theory and practice.* Second edition. London: Routledge.

Knowles, M. (1970) *The Modern Practice of Adult Education.* New York: Associated Press.

Polanyi, M. (1966) *The Tacit Dimension.* London: Routledge.

Rogers, J. (2007) *Adults Learning.* Fifth edition. Buckingham: Open University Press.

Schön, D. (1983) *The Reflective Practitioner: how professionals think in action*. Aldershot: Ashgate.

Shulman, L. (1986) Those who understand: knowledge growth in teaching. *Educational Researcher*, 15(2): 4–14.

Stevenson, J. (2002) Concepts of workplace knowledge. *International Journal of Educational Research,* 37(1): 1–15.

Tummons, J. (2007) *Becoming a Professional Tutor in the Lifelong Learning Sector*. Exeter: Learning Matters.

Websites

Details about the BTEC award can be found at:
www.edexcel.org.uk/quals/nat/engineering/cert/4322/

Details about the NCFE award can be found at:
www.ncfe.org.uk/Default.aspx?modhash=nvqinadvice-guidance

7
A universal curriculum?
Every Child Matters, and education for sustainable development

By the end of this chapter you should:

- be able to describe and evaluate the role played by *Every Child Matters* within the wider curriculum in the lifelong learning sector;
- have an increased awareness of the issues and debates that surround the concept of the sustainable curriculum.

Professional Standards

This chapter relates to the following Professional Standards:

Professional Values:

AS 2 Learning, its potential to benefit people emotionally, intellectually, socially and economically, and its contribution to community sustainability.

AS 3 Equality, diversity and inclusion in relation to learners, the workforce, and the community.

Professional Knowledge and Understanding:

AK 2.2 Ways in which learning promotes the emotional, intellectual, social and economic well-being of individuals and the population as a whole.

AK 3.1 Issues of equality, diversity and inclusion.

Professional Practice:

AP 2.2 Encourage learners to recognise and reflect on ways in which learning can empower them as individuals and make a difference in their communities.

AP 3.1 Apply principles to evaluate and develop own practice in promoting equality and inclusive learning and engaging with diversity.

This chapter will allow you to work towards the following elements of the *LLUK Minimum Core:*

Language and Literacy – Personal Language Skills
Reading:

- Find, and select from, a range of reference material and sources of information, including the internet.
- Use and reflect on a range of reading strategies to interpret texts and to locate information or meaning.
- Identify and record the key information or messages contained within reading material using note-taking techniques.

Introduction

Some things are considered so important that they should be embedded within all curricula. That is to say, there are some things that everybody should know or understand and therefore they need to be a part of the educational experience that everyone receives. And these things can be described as relating to everybody: as being universal. This is not the same thing as, for example, the National Curriculum, which is an attempt to create a unified approach to the study of those subjects that are deemed to be of central importance for schoolchildren to learn. (Friends of mine who work in schools argue about how effective this is, but such a debate is certainly outside the scope of this book.) When talking about a universal aspect of curriculum, I mean to draw attention to those themes, issues or approaches that are being included within curriculum planning across different educational sectors generally, and the lifelong learning sector in particular (the focus of this book). This is a time-sensitive issue: some of the themes that we will discuss in this chapter simply did not exist a few years ago in the same way that they do now and, as we shall see, the impetus for some of the issues that we will cover in this chapter is of relatively recent origin. These are also political issues as well: the themes that we will look at are not always accepted without debate.

Some opening remarks about a universal curriculum

What do I mean when I talk about a universal curriculum? I am using this term to describe the idea that some things – issues, topics, subjects – are seen as being so important that they have to be included at some level in all of the different specialist areas that make up the curriculum. Within the context of this book, as well as of a programme of teacher training leading to QTLS, our focus is on the curriculum that is delivered within the learning and skills sector, although the argument for a universal curriculum can be extended both to compulsory schooling and to Higher Education as well. A straightforward, and easily recognisable, example of a universal curriculum component would be functional skills (as discussed in Chapter 3, where a definition can also be found). Functional skills are seen as being so important in so many different aspects of life (work, social, family, personal) that a key aim of the education system must be to allow students to develop them.

This is not to say that the place of functional skills within the post-compulsory curriculum is taken for granted. There are several different theoretical and practical perspectives that might raise questions about the ways in which functional skills are delivered, embedded, or even defined. Indeed, even the actual concept of 'functional skills' is questioned by some researchers and practitioners. But the consensus relating to functional skills is so strong (not least because of the political as well as economic impetus that lies behind it) that their application across curricular contexts is virtually unchallenged. As a result, we can see functional skills as well as earlier conceptions such as key skills, across educational sectors, including Higher Education: those people who are reading this book while working towards QTLS will be aware of the language, literacy and numeracy requirements that are embedded within the teacher-training curriculum for the learning and skills sector.

This chapter consists of two in-depth case studies which seek to explore the ways in which universal curricular themes are formed, championed and then applied in practical settings. The two case studies that have been chosen are both backed up by considerable political and educational arguments, and are both applicable across different educational contexts. Our two case studies are *Every Child Matters* (ECM) and Education for Sustainable Development (ESD). ECM is a well-publicised government strategy, and as such only needs a relatively short introduction here. ESD is less identifiable, and will require a somewhat more detailed analysis.

Every Child Matters

Every Child Matters (ECM) is the name given to the UK government's agenda for children and young adults under the age of 19 and for vulnerable adults up to the age of 25. In this context, vulnerable adults are defined as adults with learning difficulties or disabilities, or those adults deemed at risk from social exclusion. The government's wide-reaching agenda aims to provide a coherent and comprehensive *modus operandi* for all of those bodies and agencies that are involved in services for children. This includes not only education services, but health and welfare services as well. The Children Act of 2004, together with the publication of *Every Child Matters: Change for Children* provide the most accessible starting points for those wishing to explore the detail that underpins ECM (although it should be noted that *Every Child Matters: Change for Children* itself draws on over 20 other relevant government reports and publications). The death of Victoria Climbié is generally highlighted as one of the main drivers for the *Every Child Matters* strategy, although many of the issues and themes covered by ECM were in existence before this time.

Every Child Matters rests on five central outcomes (each of which has a number of sub-themes) that are defined as being essential to the growth and development (in the widest sense) of children and young adults:

1. being healthy;
2. staying safe;
3. enjoying and achieving;
4. making a positive contribution;
5. achieving economic well-being.

These themes are additionally defined as being central to the work of all educational institutions, other than those that deal exclusively with the education of adults. As such, they have been integrated into the Ofsted Common Inspection Framework (which we shall return to shortly). At first glance, it might seem to be the case that not all of the ECM framework is relevant to the lifelong learning sector, not least because of the simple fact that the strategy is all about children and young adults up to the age of 19, and not all college-based tutors work with students aged between 14 and 16. Adult education students clearly fall outside this remit. At the same time, the fact that there is a lot of talk about 'schools' within *Every Child Matters: Change for Children* might make practitioners think that FE or work-based learning is outside the scope of the strategy. In fact, there is much to concern colleges as well as schools.

Achieving economic well-being

This provides us with the most straightforward entry to ECM, through its first sub-theme: *engage in further education, employment or training on leaving school*. This, after all, is perceived to be the core business of further education. However, a consideration of the other themes that make up ECM provides a number of relatively straightforward ways of thinking about how it impacts on the broader work that is done within mainstream FE or work-based learning (WBL).

Being healthy

This theme covers issues relating to not only physical health, but mental and emotional health as well. Therefore, within a college environment, planning is needed for the provision of a range of facilities, from healthy food and readily accessible drinking water, through to properly staffed welfare and guidance services. Aspects of the wider curriculum, such as opportunities for sport and recreation, are also covered within this theme.

Staying safe

Appropriate health and safety training is a common feature of induction programmes for both students and staff within educational institutions, as well as being a core component of many courses in the construction curriculum. But this theme also relates to the wider steps that need to be taken to maintain safety and security, for both people and their property. It also relates to the policies that colleges need to establish, and that tutors need to support, in order to ensure safety in its widest sense, such as anti-discrimination policies and anti-bullying policies.

Enjoying and achieving

Achieving is certainly a familiar word to tutors working within the learning and skills sector. Whether at a main campus or in a community setting, targets relating to attendance, progression and achievement are a common feature of daily working life. This theme relates to all those aspects of educational provision that contribute towards a positive and constructive student learning experience. Issues to consider that are directly related to teaching and learning include both good class-based teaching, and the provision of one-to-one support through tutorials and the use of Individual Learning Plans (ILPs). Relevant issues drawn from the wider curriculum include punctuality and attendance, and the opportunity for students to provide feedback relating to not only their course or programme of study, but wider features of college life.

Making a positive contribution

Here, making a positive contribution is understood as relating to the individual student both in the classroom and in the wider educational environment. In a classroom or workshop setting, students should have the opportunity to develop the confidence and ability to play a meaningful part in the learning that is taking place. A positive contribution does not refer only to classroom participation, however, but also to contribution to the life of the organisation as a whole. This might be through membership of a staff-student panel or a college council that would also include other stakeholders such as college governors and local employers. As such, a positive contribution rests on learners being aware of both their rights and their responsibilities within an educational context.

ECM and quality assurance

While *Every Child Matters* has undoubtedly done much to galvanise the delivery of education and training services (as well as other areas of provision) for children and young adults, it would be quite incorrect to suggest that either before ECM, or without it, such services would not exist or would be offered at a lower standard. When reading through the ECM framework, it quickly becomes apparent that much of what is described within it was happening anyway, and that the role of ECM is at one level simply to co-ordinate the activities of the different service providers involved. Ideas that students should be able to participate actively in learning, be able to provide meaningful feedback relating to the education and training that they are receiving, or be able to access a range of additional services relating to personal as well as academic issues, are hardly new or revolutionary. What ECM has done is to provide a new legislative framework, and hence a new government impetus, for these ideas. A further consequence of such high-profile political pressure is the introduction of rigorous quality assurance procedures to ensure that ECM is being adhered to appropriately.

Consequently, the latest version of the *Handbook for Inspecting Colleges* (published in September 2008) states:

> *Issues affecting the well-being of learners have always been central to inspection judgements. They are now more significant following the Children Act 2004. Clearly it is not the sole responsibility of schools and colleges to ensure that children and young people achieve these outcomes. However, they play a part, along with other local services, in facilitating their well-being. Consequently, inspectors will evaluate and grade the extent to which the... five outcomes for children and young people up to the age of 25 are being met.*
>
> (Ofsted, 2008, p61)

With the ECM framework now within Ofsted's remit, it is unsurprising to learn that it has also found its way into other quality assurance systems and processes within educational institutions. College Self Assessment Reports (SARs), which themselves have to be submitted to Ofsted prior to an inspection taking place, now need to take account of ECM. ECM is now a common feature of staff induction events as well as more general continuing professional development. In some institutions, ECM themes are included within institutional scheme of work and lesson plan templates.

There are clear advantages as well as disadvantages to such an approach. At one level, the ECM themes could be seen quite simply as being another way of describing the work that tutors and colleges already do – so why do we need another government initiative on top of all the other ones that we have to deal with? More specifically, as soon as any aspect of the tutor's professional practice becomes a component of a target-driven audit culture, the possibility of resistance or non-compliance arises. By this I do not mean to say that tutors will start wilfully acting in such a way that their working practices will somehow disadvantage students or deliberately exclude them. Rather, there is a risk that tutors' perceptions of, and reactions to, the ECM agenda will revolve around the paperwork and audit trail that has sprung up around it, rather than the actual key outcomes (about which there can surely be no significant disagreement) that the agenda puts forward. Similarly, the ways in which tutors respond to Ofsted inspections, which can be described as sometimes stressful at the very least, might have a consequent impact on the ways in which tutors respond to ECM. It would be a pity indeed if an excessive concern with regulation and bureaucracy led to the central message of ECM being lost sight of.

Overall, however, it can be argued that the *Every Child Matters* agenda has been integrated into the working practices of the learning and skills sector as a whole. Our second universal curriculum theme, education for sustainable development, is perhaps less high profile.

Education for sustainable development

At first glance, there might not seem to be much in common between a scheme whereby staff who work in a further education college can receive a tax incentive that encourages them to buy a bicycle to come to work on, and the BTEC National Certificate in Electrical and Electronic Engineering which we explored in the previous chapter. In fact, they both embody aspects of the same broader theme: environmental and social awareness and sustainability. Encouraging staff to cycle to work (or, alternatively, to use public transport) is just one way by which a further education college can encourage an institutional ethos of environmental sustainability. And the BTEC course includes a unit called 'business systems for technicians', the content for which includes the study of the environmental impact of a typical engineering company. And so we arrive at the concept of education for sustainable development: education which provides an awareness and understanding of society's overlapping environmental, economic and social needs and responsibilities.

At the time of writing this book, it seems to be entirely uncontroversial to say that environmental issues are of the utmost importance to us all. The actual steps taken by the political classes to help curb some of the more environmentally damaging aspects of our lives may be variable in terms of impact and conviction, but the broader principle is well established. And so when we go shopping, we are encouraged to buy a reusable shopping bag. Doorstep recycling collections are commonplace. When we go on holiday, we are asked to calculate our carbon footprint, and to offset the pollution caused by our air travel through paying for the planting of trees. The media is replete with information and stories about global climate change and consequent environmental impact. For the purposes of this discussion, the question is: how do these broader concerns lead to the publication in 2005, by the Learning and Skills Council, of a paper called 'From here to sustainability: the Learning and Skills Council's strategy for sustainable development', and the correlating identification of sustainable development as an economic need in 'Skills in England 2007', also published by the LSC?

CLOSE FOCUS **CLOSE** FOCUS **CLOSE** FOCUS **CLOSE** FOCUS **CLOSE** FOCUS

A timeline for sustainability in the lifelong learning sector

There are a number of key dates and publications to consider that lead up to the current focus on environmental and sustainable development within the sector:

1993 – Environmental Responsibility: an agenda for further and higher education

This report came a year after the Rio Earth Summit which led to a large-scale international agreement about reducing greenhouse gases (the Kyoto Protocol). In it, several recommendations were made for introducing an environmental agenda into further and higher education, including both the creation of new courses that would provide specifically environmental qualifications, and the 'greening' of the existing curriculum for both new students and those already in the workforce.

1998 – Opportunities for All (DfEE)

The Department for Education and Employment (as it was then known) used this publication to set out key objectives for sustainable development, including the effective protection of the environment and the prudent use of natural resources.

1998 – Sustainable Development Education Panel

The first annual report of the Sustainable Development Education Panel established a number of key targets for further and higher education institutions, to be met by 2010. These targets included ensuring that staff were fully trained in sustainable development, the provision of relevant ESD learning opportunities to all students, and college accreditation to recognised sustainable development management systems.

1999 – Towards Sustainability: a guide for colleges (AOC/FEDA)

Written in response to the Sustainable Development Education Panel report, this document outlined a series of strategies and indicators for embedding sustainability within the work of the FE sector. Indicators included targets for management (for example, the publication and wide dissemination of a college sustainability policy), teachers (for example, relevant professional development) and students (for example, student engagement in relevant local community projects).

2005 – Securing the Future: delivering the UK sustainable development strategy

This UK Government document outlined a comprehensive series of strategies and commitments relating to environmental and sustainable development. Key themes covered included business and economic responsibilities (for example, the reduction of waste and harmful emissions), as well as community-based targets (for example, relating to land use or environmental improvement in deprived areas).

2006 – From Here To Sustainabilty (LSC)

In this key document, the LSC set out five distinct areas for curriculum development within the learning and skills sector: the promotion of education for sustainable development; the use of appropriate learning materials; the need for a whole-institution approach; the need for links and partnerships with other stakeholders; and the importance of healthy college programmes.

2007 – Skills in England (LSC)

The 2007 edition of 'Skills in England' identified the economic impetus of sustainable development, but also went on to caution that for the most part, the exact skills that would be needed within the UK economy in order to meet this challenge have yet to be satisfactorily identified.

Lifelong learning, curriculum and education for sustainable development: barriers

The central themes of sustainable development certainly appear to be well established in public life generally. There has been considerable activity by the government as well as by several key stakeholders within educational contexts: the LSC, the National Institute for Adult and Continuing Education (NIACE) and the Higher Education Academy (HEA) have all published policy papers relating to education for sustainable development (ESD). But there is still quite a way to travel from the political push to encourage ESD into the curriculum, towards an application of ESD that is relevant, authentic and meaningful. How can ESD be made sense of in a curriculum that is as diverse and as complex as that which is found in the lifelong learning sector? Recent literature and research highlights several possible barriers (some of which overlap to some degree) to the integration of ESD in the curriculum.

National Occupational Standards

As we discussed in Chapter 2, many vocational, technical and professional curricula rest either on National Occupational Standards or on other standards relating to occupational competence, such as professional codes of practice. Such standards may also be linked to legislative requirements. At a purely practical level one factor that prevents ESD from becoming more widely represented in the curriculum is the fact that in many areas (though by no means all) it has not been widely perceived as occupationally relevant and therefore does not find its way into the range statements or assessment criteria of many qualifications. At a time when educational provision across sectors is perceived as increasingly being driven by assessment targets at the expense of a more holistic approach to learning, it would seem difficult to envision a broad application of ESD within the curriculum without a target culture to reinforce it.

An already crowded curriculum

Another concern for practitioners is the fact that in the lifelong learning sector generally, there simply isn't sufficient room for ESD. This problem can be seen as working at different levels within different sectors. In mainstream FE, the very full workload of the tutor (which includes both teaching and administrative issues), together with existing requirements to embed functional or key skills, and provide both tutorial and broader welfare support, leave little room for the inclusion of ESD. In adult and community education, tutor workload issues are compounded by the fact that they may only be with their students for one or two classes each week.

Attitudes of staff, students and other stakeholders

With such pressures on time, it is not too surprising to learn that teaching staff are reluctant or unsure about embedding ESD in the curriculum. This is not to say that they lack an understanding of the issues involved. But at the end of the day, the learning and skills sector values results: enrolment, progression and achievement. The performance-driven culture of not only FE but adult education as well has led to a concentration on results that leaves little room for any kind of activity that is not seen as being directly related to the assessment and hence to the award or qualification itself. The impact that such a focus on assessment has on the broader teaching process is sometimes referred to as 'curriculum creep' – an appropriate term in the context of this book. So if staff are focused solely on results – as a consequence of management cultures and funding regimes – where does that leave ESD? Similarly, as education and training is more and more seen to be a commodity (the 'marketisation' of education), students, employers and other stakeholders have less and less time for studying (or for paying people to study) course content that is not directly related to the qualification. At the other end of the scale, students on a non-accredited or recreational programme would undoubtedly feel that any time not spent on the actual course content would represent poor use of time as well as money.

Staff awareness and expertise

Over the last few years, I have spoken with many tutors working in mainstream FE who have also had responsibility for delivering key skills to their students in addition to their 'main' subject areas. Sometimes, these tutors have been quite happy to add key skills to their teaching workloads. At other times, however, the tutors have been less confident. For some tutors, delivering key skills is difficult because their own underpinning knowledge is less than sufficient. Relevance is also an important factor to consider: it can be difficult for tutors who are working to embed key skills always to come up with meaningful and authentic examples or exercises. And as the new agenda for functional skills takes effect, the need for all tutors to understand if not actually teach them becomes more important. This is why teachers working towards QTLS now have to follow the minimum core for language, literacy and numeracy. The same issues relating to expertise, relevance and understanding apply to ESD. So how can tutors be expected to learn about it, and to embed it into their programmes of study? Will an ESD component be the next example of curriculum reform for QTLS?

Institutional commitment

It is not an exaggeration to say that tutors in the lifelong learning sector have varying degrees of professional autonomy. In non-accredited adult education tutors enjoy more freedom of action, in terms of curriculum design and delivery, than is the case for tutors in a large further education college. Without the impetus of an awarding body or a funding agency, however, it seems unlikely that adult education tutors would feel any institutional pressure to embed ESD within their curricula. FE tutors, by contrast, are only too used to responding to the pressures of working within a regimented environment. So if ESD is to become a reality then it stands to reason that a significant role needs to be played by colleges, awarding bodies and funding agencies. In turn, these institutions respond to government. The frequency of successive governments' activity in education and training has already been commented on in this book. So the real question is: will government push the ESD agenda with the same vigour that it has championed the new 14–19 diplomas (which, at the time of writing this book, have so far received a somewhat muted response)?

Lifelong learning, curriculum and ESD: responses

Clearly, the identification of a range of potential barriers to ESD planning and participation does not mean that the project should be shelved. Rather, creative and innovative responses need to be found that will allow what might be termed the ESD ethic to find its way into the curriculum. We shall look at some specific examples of how ESD has been successfully embedded within different vocational and professional curricula. But first we need to think in broader terms about how to overcome the barriers that we have identified. Current research and literature tends to focus on a number of themes, set out below.

Rethinking learning and teaching

This sounds ambitious, and it is. But this is not a call for a fundamental 'root and branch' rethink of what we think learning and teaching actually are (which is not to say that such a rethink isn't needed, because it might be). Rather, it is an attempt to consider how environmental and sustainable issues or themes might underpin all aspects of our work as educators in just the same way that they cut across all kinds of different sectors of employment, whether that might be industry or commerce, in the public or private sectors. This isn't just a job for front-line teaching staff: if we, as teachers and trainers, are going to promulgate the ESD ethic, then we need awarding bodies to design or amend curricula so that we have an opportunity to do so. At the same time, we need to identify those aspects of existing curricula that will support the ESD approach. In some ways, the other responses to the ESD challenge that appear below can all be seen as starting from this point.

Educators as role models

Role-modelling is just one theoretical approach to learning and teaching, but it is particularly apposite in this context. If teachers and trainers across curricula can be seen to be enacting those aspects of the ESD ethic that are most relevant to them and to their areas of specialism and competence, then the process of 'greening' the curriculum will be facilitated.

Experiential learning

Experiential learning is another useful teaching and learning concept upon which we can draw in this context. If we assume that authentic, real-life experiences can provide meaningful opportunities for learning, then it follows that by creating opportunities for students to take part in activities that embody particular aspects of ESD – as opposed to just talking about them – there will be a greater opportunity for learning.

A whole-institution approach

The sustainable curriculum is not just about what goes on in the workshop or classroom, however. For an ESD ethic to underpin all aspects of our working lives, it needs to be embedded within not only our philosophies of learning and teaching, but also the ethos of the institution for which we work. Without the support and leadership of college managers, a sustainable curriculum will be difficult to achieve.

Teaching the sustainable curriculum

Now that we have rehearsed the issues and debates that surround the sustainable curriculum, we are in a position to think about how it will make itself felt in the workshop or classroom. Having established the key principles that underpin an effective ESD curriculum we can now think about how these can inform our teaching practice.

As might be expected, some subject areas are so suitable for embedding ESD that they need relatively little exploration: geography, for example, or biology. Other areas of study, such as courses in sustainable land use or countryside management, are more obvious examples of how environmental and sustainable issues are impacting on education and training. And in some subject areas, awarding bodies have already begun to adapt existing curricular schemes in order to take account of ESD. Examples include the City and Guilds plumbing curriculum as well as courses in electrical engineering and travel and tourism. In fact, it would seem to be the case that ESD is making itself felt across many different curricular areas.

CLOSE FOCUS **CLOSE** FOCUS **CLOSE** FOCUS **CLOSE** FOCUS **CLOSE** FOCUS

Examples of ESD in the further education curriculum

BTEC Level 3 National Award in Countryside Management

In this programme, there is a specific unit titled 'environmental issues and policies', which includes environmental awareness, biodiversity and sustainable energy, as well as the study of relevant world events such as the *Exxon Valdez* shipping accident.

BTEC Level 2 First Certificate in Travel and Tourism

Course specifications for this qualification include an exploration of why environmental issues are important, and how environmental factors affect the UK travel and tourism industry.

City and Guilds 6129 Level 2 Certificate in Basic Plumbing Studies

This course includes a unit called 'environmental awareness in plumbing' which seeks (among other things) to make both tutors and apprentices aware of the environmental impact of their profession, beginning with relatively straightforward concerns such as the efficient use of resources so as to minimise wastage.

Enrichment activities

Enrichment activities, seen here as part of the wider FE curriculum, have been used in many institutions to help promote ESD. Examples include community-based volunteering projects, healthy college campaigns and recycling projects.

ECM and ESD: some final thoughts

Every Child Matters is to a significant degree the product of a process by which a variety of relevant service providers across different sectors (education, the voluntary sector, business, social services) have been given a unified and coherent agenda to which they are all required to work, driven by government legislation. Education for sustainable development also has considerable support. They are both clearly important, they both have an immediate impact on the provision of education and training, and they both contribute to educational, social and economic well-being in the broadest sense. But there is one crucial difference. The commitment of the government to ECM is easily attested to by the fact that Ofsted inspections now report on ECM (although this aspect of a report is not published). ESD has no such driver. In some ways this must be seen as a good thing: previous attempts to impose what might be seen as a managerialist solution to the ESD problem do not appear to have been successful. Education for sustainable development is a state of mind, not just a series of outcomes or targets and as such a target-driven approach would perhaps be undesirable (Blewitt, 2005; Bonnett, 1999).

So, what should teachers and trainers in the lifelong learning sector be doing? As far as ECM is concerned, our professional responsibility lies both in upholding the core message that it contains and in refusing to allow it to become another behaviourist or managerialist tick-box exercise: the themes that it encompasses are too important. The ESD curriculum is equally important, but without the forthright political advocacy that ECM enjoys, and one that we have an additional responsibility to provide, assuming that such a curriculum can be said to exist in a coherent sense. At this time a consensus relating to the position of ESD within the curriculum is far from settled. Conversations about global economic sustainability can seem far removed from the day-to-day experiences of apprentices in the learning and skills sector, not least when they are expressed using unfamiliar language and abstract themes such as 'globalisation', 'eco-systems' and 'food safety'.

A SUMMARY OF **KEY POINTS**

In this chapter we have looked at the following key themes:

> **the emergence of the *Every Child Matters* agenda, and its impact on policy and practice within the lifelong learning sector;**

> **debates surrounding education for sustainable development, and how it can be embedded within existing curricula.**

The undeniable importance of these issues would seem to suggest that the notion of a universal curriculum, a curriculum that everyone ought to be a participant within, is sound. But this rests on the assumption that a consensus can be reached about what such a curriculum ought to contain. The need for such a consensus raises difficult questions to do with political power (who has the right, as well as the authority, to impose a universal curriculum?) as well as teacher autonomy. To what extent should we, as professionals, feel obligated to deliver such a curriculum?

Branching options

Reflection

Every Child Matters seems to be well established within relevant areas of the lifelong learning sector, but Education for Sustainable Development has a much more tenuous position. Some of the questions that we might ask of our own teaching practice are: to what extent can or should our own teaching practices embed notions of sustainability? Do we actually have a personal sense of what sustainability means within our own lives?

Analysis

ECM and ESD, as potential aspects of a universal curriculum, would seem to be of equal importance. And yet, as has been discussed in this chapter, only one of them has enjoyed a sufficient level of immediate government advocacy and support. 'Green' politics are plentiful, but government-led projects for sustainable living seem to enjoy only partial success (such as recent government initiatives to encourage the building of sustainable 'carbon neutral' houses).

Research

The references that appear below cover both of the themes that have been explored in this chapter, although ESD has been given a higher profile. This has been done deliberately, as a reflection of the fact that at this time, it is a relatively nebulous concept. The website for *Every Child Matters: Change for Children* is recommended for those wishing to explore the background to ECM, and contains links to a number of relevant policy documents.

REFERENCES AND FURTHER READING REFERENCES AND FURTHER READING

Blewitt J. (2006) *The Ecology of Learning: sustainability, lifelong learning and everyday life.* London: Earthscan.

Blewitt, J. (2005) Education for Sustainable Development, governmentality and 'Learning to Last'. *Environmental Education Research*, 11(2): 173–185.

Bonnett, M. (1999) Education for Sustainable Development: a coherent philosophy for environmental education? *Cambridge Journal of Education*, 29(3): 313–324.

Websites

Every Child Matters – Change for Children:
www.everychildmatters.gov.uk/

Ofsted:
www.ofsted.gov.uk/Ofsted-home/Forms-and-guidance/Browse-all-by/Other/General/Handbook-for-inspecting-colleges

From Here To Sustainability:
http://readingroom.lsc.gov.uk/lsc/2005/ourbusiness/strategy/from-here-to-sustainability-lsc-strategy-for-sustainable-development.pdf

Towards Sustainability: a guide for colleges:
http://eric.ed.gov/ERICWebPortal/custom/portlets/recordDetails/detailmini.jsp?_nfpb=true&_ERICExtSearch_SearchValue_0=ED435810&ERICExtSearch_SearchType_0=no&acono=ED435810

Skills in England (2007):
http://research.lsc.gov.uk/LSC+Research/published/skills-in-england/

Securing the Future:
www.defra.gov.uk/sustainable/government/publications/uk-strategy/index.htm

The Stern Review:
www.hm-treasury.gov.uk/sternreview_index.htm

8
The accessible curriculum

By the end of this chapter you should:

- have a critical appreciation of current debates around widening participation and inclusive practice;
- have an understanding of the impact of recent legislation on the educational provision available to students with disabilities.

Professional Standards

This chapter relates to the following Professional Standards:

Professional Values:

AS 3 Equality, diversity and inclusion in relation to learners, the workforce, and the community.

Professional Knowledge and Understanding:

AK 3.1 Issues of equality, diversity and inclusion.

Professional Practice:

AP 3.1 Apply principles to evaluate and develop own practice in promoting equality and inclusive learning and engaging with diversity.

This chapter will allow you to work towards the following elements of the *LLUK Minimum Core:*

Language and Literacy – Personal Language Skills
Reading:

- **Find, and select from, a range of reference material and sources of information, including the internet.**
- **Use and reflect on a range of reading strategies to interpret texts and to locate information or meaning.**

Introduction

One of the things that I like most about further education colleges is the fact that, as institutions, they do a really good job in widening access to the courses and facilities that they provide, to students from all kinds of backgrounds, and with all kinds of profiles. Such provision, alongside the 'core' business of the mainstream further education curriculum for 16–19-year-old students, is an essential part of the mission of the sector. The teachers and trainers that I am working with, at the time of writing this book, work in a broad range of professional contexts (as described in the 'mixed teacher-training group' exercise in Chapter 4) and with a similarly wide-ranging mixture of students:

- 14–16-year-old students, in both school settings and college settings;
- mainstream FE groups, aged 16–19;

- adult learners in community settings, sometimes from disadvantaged backgrounds;
- students with significant learning difficulties and disabilities;
- apprentices on day release;
- adults learning for pleasure on a recreational basis.

Such variety of provision is what the lifelong learning sector is all about. Political and academic definitions of 'lifelong learning' change over time, as do the jobs that particular institutions within the sector carry out, usually because of changes to funding. Provision for 14–16-year-olds is a relatively recent aspect of the work of FE colleges. Adult education that is funded by local education authorities is now formally accredited through RARPA (Recognition and Recording of Progress and Achievement). The *Train to Gain* scheme (discussed in Chapter 3) was implemented nationally just two years ago.

These and other kinds of provision within the lifelong learning sector tend to be grouped together using a number of different, though familiar, headings such as 'widening participation' and 'return to learn'. At the same time, teachers and trainers are reminded of the importance of a range of pedagogic strategies that are gathered together using concepts such as 'inclusive practice' and 'differentiation', as they work with students who are described as 'diverse', 'non-traditional' or 'returners'. Some of these terms are so diffuse in meaning that they become meaningless: describing a group of students as 'diverse', for example, can only really make sense if we assume that there is such a thing as a non-diverse group of students. And while many teachers and trainers do indeed work with student groups that are sometimes stereotypically viewed as being 'mainstream' or 'homogeneous', the reality is that all of our students need, first and foremost, to be treated as individuals, and we should take account of this at all times when planning and delivering curricula. This is not an uncritical call for an 'individualised learning' approach, however. The political impetus behind 'individualised learning' is currently (thankfully) in decline, as the conceptual and theoretical difficulties that surround the term have begun at last to be taken into consideration by policy-makers. Rather, as teachers and trainers, we simply need to be sensitive to the needs, backgrounds and profiles of the students that we work with, so that we can help them work to the best of their potential within appropriate courses and programmes of study.

REFLECTIVE TASK

Defining terms

'Widening participation', 'inclusive practice', and 'differentiation' are three commonly heard – and read – terms. They are found in teacher-training books, articles and government publications. But what do they actually mean? Before reading on, consider what these terms actually mean, firstly on your own, and then in consultation with a colleague or mentor.

So what does all of this mean in real terms? Put simply, it means thinking about our teaching, and our curricula, in such a way that any student can access it to the best of their potential ability. We should stretch and challenge our students, not patronise them and dumb things down. But this stretching and challenging (which, according to one theoretical perspective, is where learning occurs) needs to be appropriately and carefully managed, so that we are helping our students to reach their potential, at whatever level that might be, while recognising that some students will be better at doing some things than others. Or, to put it another way, we need to try to make sure that each individual student works as well as they can and does the best that they can.

So how does a debate that in some senses is about being aware of students' different learning needs and aspirations and finding appropriate pedagogies for responding to them ('differentiation'), relate to students with learning difficulties and disabilities, who also featured in our wide-ranging mixture of students?

Students with disabilities: mainstream or apart?

The increased visibility of students who have specific seen or unseen disabilities, or who need other support on order to access education and training, is the product of a number of factors. Undoubtedly, legislation has played an important part in creating more accessible opportunities for students (and we shall look at the Disability Discrimination Act in more detail later on in this chapter). But changing social attitudes are also important – indeed, more so. Legislation is all well and good, but only if attitudes towards working with students with disabilities change, will the curriculum as a whole become more accessible. Legislation has ostensibly been promoting opportunities for students with disabilities for several years by the time I write this, but in the real world, provision is still far from unified. Colleges, adult education providers and awarding bodies all have policies relating to working with students with specific learning needs. But the distance between a college policy and classroom practice can be considerable, and disability awareness among tutors continues to be variable. This is not intended as a criticism or professional indictment. It is simply a reflection of the fact that for many tutors, professional training relating to working with students with specific disabilities or difficulties tends to be restricted to induction events or training days, or is treated as a discrete topic or subject within the teacher-training curriculum. Similarly, students with disabilities (seen or unseen) are too easily objectified as such: their disability becomes their defining characteristic from the point of view of the educational planning process, either because they are participating in a curriculum that has been designed solely for such a student group, or because of the many 'special measures' or 'special circumstances' policies and procedures that swing into action whenever a student with a disability or learning difficulty enrols on a so-called 'mainstream' programme of study.

Obviously it is not the case that the broader vocational or FE curriculum is equally accessible to any student with any disability. Nor is it discriminatory to say to a student with a disability that a particular course or programme of study might not be suitable for them, in the same way that it is not discriminatory to say the same thing to any other student during an advice or guidance session. It is not the job of the tutor, counsellor, or adviser to recommend uncritically that someone should and ought to enrol on a course which is patently unsuitable for them, irrespective of the pressures that are sometimes applied to ensure particular levels of recruitment. Setting students up to fail can have devastating consequences. But quite a lot of courses are suitable, and sometimes with only relatively minor adjustments: the kinds of adjustments, in a qualitative sense, that teachers and trainers have been exhorted to make, in order to be seen to be 'inclusive' and to be 'differentiating', for several years now.

Thinking about 'the accessible curriculum'

At one level, therefore, I am arguing that there is little meaningful difference between the ways in which a teacher or trainer needs to consider the differing needs and profiles of a so-called 'mainstream' group of students, and those of a group of students that might include one or more people with a disability. Consequently, as teachers and trainers, we are expected to be proactive in our planning, to take account of individual learner needs, irrespective of whether those needs stem from a specific disability or learning difficulty, or from a consideration of those social or educational background issues that contribute to a student's profile.

So, if a curriculum is to be described as accessible, certain key factors need to have been taken into consideration:

1. that the curriculum is accessible to any student who wishes to engage with it, and for whom the curriculum would be an appropriate experience;
2. that, all other things being equal, the curriculum is accessible to all of those students who meet any relevant and appropriate entry criteria (defined in the widest possible sense, including APL/APEL);
3. that awarding bodies, education providers, teachers and trainers have a shared commitment to accessibility;
4. that barriers to accessibility are defined in the broadest terms possible, and then overcome through a proactive, whole-institution approach, as opposed to a reactive, fragmented approach.

We shall cover each of these factors in turn.

An accessible and appropriate curriculum
An accessible curriculum

So what are the practical and pedagogical steps that we need to take to ensure that a curriculum is accessible?

Teaching and learning

As teachers and trainers, we need to be responsive to our students, whether they have a specific learning difficulty such as attention deficit disorder (ADD), whether they need a British Sign language (BSL) interpreter or whether they simply need to be spoken to differently today, or given a little more time to complete the assignment that is due in a few days' time, because of complications in their home lives. Whether we describe it as reflective practice, or as praxis, as thinking reflexively, or as meeting different student learning styles (although I hold many reservations about 'learning styles theory'), it is important that how we teach, and how we help our students to learn, is not fixed. Rather, it should be dynamic and fluid, not because we slavishly follow unthinking orders to include 'VAK' (a kind of learning style approach) in all of our lesson planning, but because we spend time getting to know all of our students as people, not as units labelled 'kinaesthetic learner', or 'dyslexic student'.

Resources

Our resources also need to be accessible and, as far as is practicably possible, they need to be the same for all students, unless the group profile demands otherwise. Taking the time to prepare printed materials on coloured paper and using particular fonts is of course good practice. But when a student with dyslexia is presented with a sheaf of pale pink paper, and everyone else is given white paper, attention is drawn to that student in an unacceptable way. This is not to say that all of the group necessarily need to be provided with pink handouts. But it is important to talk to the student who does need them first, to assess their feelings about and responses to their dyslexia, and the extent to which they do or do not want this aspect of their person to be widely known.

Locations and timings

If we are to make our courses and programmes of study widely open to as many people as possible, then we need to consider practical implications such as when the course is available, and where. Accessibility in this sense relates to the availability of public transport links as well as adequate car parking, or to the provision of courses that are run at times that are compatible with dropping children off at school or nursery, or at times that allow people to work as well as study because they cannot afford to study full time. Of course, not all courses can be delivered on such flexible terms and this might be for academic reasons, practical reasons, or a combination of the two. But if government agencies and funding bodies continue to be serious about their aspirations for the education and training of the population as a whole (which is not to say that I endorse the education policies of our current government) then they need to put money into the provision of flexible opportunities for learning. This might well include e-learning (often trumpeted as a panacea for widening participation), but also needs to include real education involving proper contact with a tutor as well.

Financial issues

Costing accessible education is a fraught business. As government targets and priorities ebb and flow, whole areas of the curriculum in the lifelong learning sector find themselves either enjoying an embarrassment of riches or of being pared back. ICT and computing courses seem to have settled back down to more sensible levels (although they are still plentiful). Train to Gain is, at the time of writing this book, receiving considerable political as well as financial support. Many courses offer concessions of one kind or another. Many institutions offer hardship funds or similar. Some employers are willing to contribute to the financial cost of their employees' professional development. Nonetheless, the reality of financial cost in order to pursue a programme of study is unavoidable in many cases.

An appropriate curriculum

Having considered whether or not a curriculum is being provided for a hypothetical student in an accessible way, we need to consider whether or not the curriculum is appropriate for the student in question. Describing something as appropriate does simplify things, and this term does need to be unpacked.

A common feature of many teacher-training books and courses (and their assignments) is an analysis of the reasons why people take part in learning, whether on a full-time basis in a large further education college, or on a part-time basis in their place of work. Such discussions tend to revolve around intrinsic motivators (such as: seeking a personal challenge; enjoyment of learning) as well as extrinsic motivators (for example: needing a qualification in order to gain or keep a job; needing to obtain one qualification as a 'gateway' to studying for another).

So what makes a curriculum appropriate? Sometimes, a curriculum – in the sense of being a programme of study that has been designed and accredited by an institution or awarding body – assumes particular things about the students that might take part, usually (though not always) expressed as entry criteria. If the student meets these criteria (and this is explored more fully below), then we can assume that the programme is appropriate for them. But many programmes of study do not have formal entry criteria. Within the adult and community education sectors, such criteria are relatively rare and sometimes opposed on the grounds that they are not compatible with the 'open door' philosophy of adult education that stretches back over a hundred years. The Workers' Educational Association (WEA) maintains such a policy today. ESOL classes by their very nature need to be freely available within appropriate communities. Some programmes within the mainstream FE sector have criteria that are quite broad, and that rely on the application of the admission tutor's professional judgement in order to ensure that people don't end up on the wrong course. A decision over appropriateness might rest on explicit criteria or on the implicit criteria that a tutor draws on when making a decision. So what kind of factors will an admissions tutor take into consideration?

Accessible entry criteria

Entry criteria for a course or programme of study can vary in shape but tend to take the form of a list of required prerequisites, normally involving qualifications already held, or relevant work experience. One way by which institutions can make their programmes available to as wide an audience as is feasible is through providing flexible entry criteria. This might be done through establishing a tariff of relevant prior qualifications that would allow prospective students to apply for a place on the course on the basis of already holding one of several different combinations of qualifications. Another possible route is through giving recognition for learning that may have taken place on other unrelated courses or indeed in non-educational contexts.

CASE STUDY

HND/HNC in Sports Studies (awarded by UCLAN)

This HND/HNC in Sports Studies, which is offered at a number of further education colleges in the north-west of England, provides an excellent example of flexible entry routes.

For students with qualifications, different combinations are recognised:

- A Level applicants are expected to offer a minimum of 40 points at A2.
- AVCE (Advanced Vocational Certificate of Education) applicants are normally expected to gain a Grade E at least.
- BTEC National Diploma applicants are expected to have gained a Merit overall.
- Access to Higher Education applicants are expected to have gained a Pass grade or above.

For students without these qualifications, a flexible entry route is established through accrediting prior learning:

- Applications from prospective students with non-standard qualifications, who can demonstrate the ability to cope with and benefit from the course, are welcomed.
- Applicants who have relevant professional qualifications, work or life experience, will also be welcomed and will receive careful individual consideration.

CASE STUDY

NVQs in the automotive industry (levels 1–3)

City and Guilds are one of the awarding bodies who offer NVQs at levels 1, 2 and 3 for vehicle fitting, maintenance and repair, body and paint work, and roadside assistance.

For NVQ candidates at level 1, no specific prior qualifications, learning or experience are asked for. More generic skills are needed, however: basic literacy and numeracy skills are required, and candidates must have the ability to read and interpret written tasks, and to write in a legible and understandable manner. While direct entry at any level is possible, the awarding body recommends that candidates for the level 3 award already possess the level 2 award or equivalent practical, work-based experience. For those candidates without formal qualifications, an initial assessment should be used to diagnose their learning needs as well as assess their current abilities.

APEL and APL

Mapping the value of individual qualifications is (in theory) a straightforward task thanks to the establishment of the National Qualifications Framework (which is due to be replaced by the Qualifications and Credit Framework). Recognising other qualifications, or giving a value to work or life experience, is a little more complicated and deserves a brief mention here.

The accreditation of prior *experiential* learning (APEL) provides students with the opportunity to receive recognition for learning that has resulted from prior work and life experience, and allows institutions to give credit for what has been learned. APEL can be based on different types of evidence, such as achievement in the workplace (letters, documents or other materials demonstrating workplace responsibilities), references or testimonials written by employers, clients or customers, or evidence from community or voluntary activities. The accreditation of prior learning (APL) refers to prior learning that has been accredited and where a certificate, or other formal record of achievement, has been awarded on successful completion.

The willingness of an institution to recognise that applicants without the standard entry qualifications would be suitable for, and would benefit from, taking part in a particular course shows the widening participation ethic at work. This is important not only because in itself it constitutes equitable practice, but because for some groups of students who are often described as 'marginalised' or 'at risk', educational disadvantage can be endemic, and they may have been unable to take advantage of educational opportunities until now. Similarly, students with some disabilities often find themselves marginalised when in mainstream education, and so flexible entry policies are particularly appropriate for them. (I have lost count of the number of times that my teacher-training students have told me that they are working with students who have only been diagnosed as having dyslexia when starting at further education college.)

A shared commitment to accessibility

The increased acceptance of non-standard qualifications and APEL/APL has contributed significantly to widening participation in post-compulsory education over recent years. While entry criteria are undoubtedly important for many qualifications, they are increasingly framed in terms that can be negotiated. For students with seen or unseen disabilities, however, access to education remains more broadly problematic. Although social attitudes towards disability have changed over recent years, it is undoubtedly the case that the Disability Discrimination Act (DDA) (DDA, 1995) and its subsequent extension to include educational establishments (2003) has had a significant impact on provision in the lifelong learning sector.

The DDA impacts on policy and practice in the lifelong learning sector in a number of ways.

1. It is unlawful to discriminate against disabled students by treating them less favourably than others.
2. Responsible bodies (awarding bodies, college corporations, adult education providers) are required to provide certain types of reasonable adjustments to provision where disabled students might otherwise be substantially disadvantaged.
3. Responsible bodies are required to arrange for the provision of additional services.
4. Responsible bodies have a duty to make reasonable adjustments to physical features of buildings where these put disabled students at a disadvantage.

And there are two other key factors to bear in mind when considering the impact of the DDA:

1. Students are not obliged to tell anyone that they have a disability. Admissions forms always have a space for this, but the information can be refused. (Another issue to consider is the extent to which admissions forms are physically designed in such a way that they are in themselves accessible.)
2. It is possible for a student with a disability to feel that they have been discriminated against even if they have not revealed the disability.

This legal framework is not meant to be oppressive, however. At all times, it is important to stress the concept of reasonableness. The DDA only ever requires institutions and individuals to make reasonable adjustments – to the exterior of buildings, to course materials, to assessment practices and to classrooms and workshops. Nor should teachers and trainers feel that they alone are responsible for negotiating access to a curriculum for a student with a specific disability. In fact, the most important thing to do is to seek out appropriate specialist advice, from (for example) learning support officers, awarding bodies, disability action groups and, of course, the students themselves.

Awarding bodies, providers and individual tutors have particular responsibilities, therefore, and respond accordingly. Awarding bodies invariably have policies and guidance structures in place for when a student with a disability enrols on a particular programme. Sometimes only minor adjustments are required, such as additional time to complete an assignment. At other times more complex measures are required, such as the provision of assistive technologies (one of the undeniable benefits of Information Learning Technology). Education providers have written policies in place that detail what students with disabilities can expect from the institution. Sometimes this might be part of a college charter, sometimes a separate document. The responsibility of the tutor, in the first instance, is to learn where to go for specialist help, and to talk to the student in question. Invariably, they will have the best sense of what their needs are likely to be.

Overcoming barriers to accessibility

To some extent, much of the discussion to this point has been about locating or defining particular issues or problems, and then fixing them. This is an understandable response to the enrolment on a course of a student with particular requirements, irrespective of whether those requirements are rooted in a physical disability, the student's private life or the demands of the student's employers. Further education colleges and adult education centres are well versed in putting measures in place so that a student or group of students can enrol on a particular programme of study. Welfare officers can help students with family problems. Learning support officers can help students with disabilities apply for funding to allow them to purchase IT or other accessibility equipment. BSL interpreters will take the time to explain to tutors how best they can work together for the benefit of a student who is deaf. At a technical level, many colleges work extremely well to ensure equality of opportunity for students.

Barriers are not only logistical, organisational or financial: they are also conceptual, even philosophical. By this I mean that although at a practical or technical level, the opportunities for students with disabilities improve year on year, an attitudinal shift is still needed so that we, as teachers and trainers, can gain an insight into those aspects of society at large, and the lifelong learning sector in particular, that are inaccessible, and that do continue to throw up barriers: that are, in a word, disabling. It could be argued that a fundamental shift has occurred during the past 60 years regarding (for example) the kind of student who should aspire to going into higher education, and the kind of subjects that they should be able to study. How about a similar paradigm shift relating to students with disabilities?

Medical and social models of disability

The social model of disability puts its focus not on an individual, and thereby on any physical or mental disability that the person might have (which is what the medical model of disability does), but on the society within which they live. For example, a student who uses a wheelchair would, through the lens of the medical model of disability, be perceived as being disabled because their legs do not work and so they have to use a wheelchair in order to get around. Because this is seen as being not normal in a physical sense (that is, 'normal' people can use their legs to walk around), then the diagnosis of disability rests on the physical condition of the individual. Under the medical model of disability, the emphasis is on using assistive technology to help the disabled person fit into the world as it exists around them.

The social model works very differently. It begins with the concept that there is nothing inherently disabling about being a wheelchair user. The reasons why people using a wheelchair find it difficult to access public transport have nothing to do with the fact that they are in a wheelchair; it is because buses have not been designed in such a way that wheelchair users can get on. It is the fact of the way that buses are designed, not the fact that the wheelchair user's legs do not work, that creates the barrier. If our physical environments were designed in such a way that wheelchair users could go to the same places that people who walk can go to, then some of the disabling aspects of our world would be removed. Under the social model of disability, the emphasis is on changing the world around us so that we can all participate in it.

So, as teachers and trainers, we can adopt a social model of disability. In this way the focus moves on from thinking about how we might need to redesign our teaching activities, in order to meet the needs of a particular student with a disability, to thinking about the extent to which our curricula (with all that the term implies: teaching, resources, institutions, environments) can be made more *equitable* and more *accessible*.

Part-time tutors and the accessible curriculum

There is one final point to raise relating to the accessible curriculum: the professional role of the tutor, and the institution within which they work. For a full-time or part-time tutor in a busy further education college, finding out about the services that can be offered to students with disabilities, or with financial worries, is a pretty straightforward task. For part-time tutors working in community education settings, accessing such facilities can be more difficult. Many colleges have outreach centres, and these are effective and valuable aspects of FE provision. But they do not enjoy the same level of support service that the main college site can offer. As such, tutors in these contexts have additional pressures and responsibilities. These responsibilities are exacerbated in the tutor is employed on an hourly-paid basis, rather than on a permanent full-time or fractional contract.

A SUMMARY OF **KEY POINTS**

In this chapter we have looked at the following key themes:

> **the ways in which key terms such as widening participation, inclusive practice and differentiation are used;**

> **defining accessibility within the context of curriculum studies;**

> **the impact of the Disability Discrimination Act on educational provision since 2003.**

Thinking about curricula in terms of accessibility is a difficult task. My own reflections on the curricula within which I work (teacher training for the lifelong learning sector) lead me to conclude that in this curriculum, there is scope for improvement. To take just one example: the minimum core for language, literacy, numeracy and ICT. These apply to all teachers working towards QTLS, including English for speakers of other language (ESOL) teachers. How is this requirement going to impact on someone who is deaf and who works as a teacher of British Sign Language, their first language? Will they be allowed or able to study towards QTLS in the future?

Branching options
Reflection

What are your experiences of working with students with seen or unseen disabilities, or with students who have had to overcome other institutional, organisational or social barriers? To what extent do you feel that you were supported by your colleagues, institution, or other specialists? To what extent do you think that the key messages of *Every Child Matters*, as discussed in the previous chapter, might impact on what we have looked at in this chapter?

Analysis

Any consideration of the needs of students (whether they relate to disability, social or familial background, or anything else for that matter) eventually has to take account of the critiques of what is termed therapeutic education. Put very simply, there is a danger that we, as educationalists, spend so much time worrying about student needs or self-esteem, that we lose sight of the main purpose of our work: to challenge and stretch our students. This is a legitimate concern. As such, it is important to remember that an accessible curriculum rests on one key concept: making curricula available to anyone who wants to access it, and for whom the curriculum in question is both legitimate and appropriate.

Research

Widening access to post-compulsory education, and the broader benefits that can accrue, are well represented in literature, and some suggestions for further reading appear below. This is a big topic, covering sometimes complex educational, political and social issues, and as such does deserve a closer focus than can be afforded here.

REFERENCES AND FURTHER READING

National Institute for Adult Continuing Education (2003) *New Rights To Learn: a tutor guide to teaching adults after the Disability Discrimination Act Part 4*. Leicester: NIACE.

Preston, J. and Hammond, C. (2002) *The Wider Benefits of Further Education: practitioner views.* London: Centre for Research on the Wider benefits of Learning.

Sanderson, A. (2001) Disabled Students in Transition: a tale of two sectors' failure to communicate. *Journal of Further and Higher Education*, 25 (2): 227–240.

Thomas, L. (2001) *Widening participation in Post-Compulsory Education.* London: Continuum.

Websites

Details about the minimum core for language, literacy, numeracy and ICT can be found at:
www.lluk.org/nrp/teachersofos/3043.htm

Afterword

'Curriculum studies' is a problematic term. Definitions of curriculum vary to such an extent that a book about curriculum studies can legitimately range from coverage of quite technical matters, such as how to construct and sequence a scheme of work, to detailed political and sociological critiques of educational provision, funding and structure. Studying curriculum can involve thinking about learning and knowledge, about students and teachers, about class and society, and about government and economy. With such a wide remit, 'curriculum studies' seems a somewhat inadequate descriptor for a body of literature that focuses on the very heart and purpose of education more generally.

So, what is curriculum studies for or about, and why is it both relevant and important to a trainee teacher or tutor working towards QTLS? One answer to this question, that I hope emerges from this book, is that by thinking about the courses that we teach beyond the confines of our classrooms and workshops, we can come to an understanding of some of the influences that shape our working lives, the things that we teach, the ways we assess and the students we work with. Some of these influences will be undeniably positive and perhaps even benign, whereas others may be more educationally or socially divisive: there's plenty of room for debate. There's more to curriculum studies than just 'the curriculum', in so far as we have a common understanding of what 'curriculum' means. While there is undeniably a coherent and bounded body of scholarship that can be referred to as 'curriculum theory', other aspects of curriculum studies are perhaps best described as being in a state of flux, variously drawing on history, sociology, economics and politics (rather like the study of education more generally, in fact).

And so this book is offered as a contribution to a much wider debate. It aims to make the field of curriculum studies navigable to a wider audience. It also has a quite pragmatic aspect: the successful negotiation of the relevant aspects of the LLUK framework and the curriculum modules that are found in CertEd/PGCE or DTLLS programmes. Busy and time-pressed tutors who are working towards their QTLS qualifications sometimes lack the energy or opportunity to explore critically some of the issues raised in their teacher-training courses. But the study of the curriculum is worth the effort, as it casts a light across so many aspects of our professional lives.